the return of edgar cayce

As transcribed by C. Terry Cline, Jr.

Other works by C. Terry Cline, Jr.

Damon

Death Knell

Cross Current

Mindreader

Missing Persons

The Attorney Conspiracy

Prey

Quarry

Reaper

the return of edgar cayce

As transcribed by C. Terry Cline, Jr.

MACADAM CAGE

MacAdam/Cage Publishing
155 Sansome Street, Suite 550
San Francisco, CA 94104

www.macadamcage.com

Library of Congress Cataloging-in-Publication Data

Cayce, Edgar, 1877-1945 (Spirit)
The return of Edgar Cayce / as transcribed by C. Terry Cline, Jr.
p. cm.
ISBN 978-1-59692-374-4 (hardcover)
1. Cayce, Edgar, 1877-1945. 2. Parapsychology. 3. Prophecies
(Occultism) 4. Forecasting. I. Cline, C. Terry. II. Title.
BF1040.C385 2011
133.9'3—dc23
2011050211

Book design by Dorothy Carico Smith

Printed in the United States of America

First edition.

10 9 8 7 6 5 4 3 2 1

Dedicated to
Marilyn Dinner-Sietz
Seymour Sietz

and to Bills I can never repay for enduring friendship:
Bill Adams
Bill Suttlemyre
Bill Ross
And as always, to Judith Richards and Linda Cline

Thanks to Donna de Vries and Charlotte Jones Cabaniss
Robertson for editing with sharp eyes for commas,
grammar, and other elusive little details

—Foreword—

Ibecame interested in Edgar Cayce during the mid-sixties. I was flying to New York City with a layover in Georgia. An acquaintance in Atlanta gave me a book titled *Edgar Cayce on Atlantis*. She said the text had upset her and she wanted my opinion of the thoughts in that tome, specifically concerning reincarnation.

I read the book on the plane; for three days I stayed in my NYC hotel room and read continuously. What did I think? I thought Mr. Cayce had revealed my inner thoughts about a lot of things, including Atlantis. Was this fellow for real?

Thus began a fifty-year odyssey in search of Edgar Cayce, the so-called sleeping prophet.

According to what I read about him, if he was given

a person's location anywhere in the world, he could diagnose that person's medical problems and then offer advice for a cure. He achieved this by lying down, closing his eyes, folding his hands across his abdomen, and entering a hypnotic trance, as though sleeping. During the self-induced sleep he claimed to reach the Universal Wave where time and distance had no meaning. These sessions were referred to as readings, and for forty-three years of his adult life Edgar Cayce answered questions sent to him. Sometimes the topic would be a life-threatening illness—other cases would be as simple as getting rid of warts or overcoming a balding head.

He spoke of auras, soul mates, and universal laws that ruled the lives of mankind. Now and then he was asked to give readings regarding career opportunities, marital problems, and the difficulty of raising children. Nothing was too far afield to be considered. He delved into politics, fortune hunting, and human relations. If asked, he answered. What kind of hoax was this?

I went to Selma, Alabama, where he'd worked as a photographer. I met his barber and neighbors who had lived next door, people for whom he had done medical readings, members of his church, a woman who knew his wife.

In Hopkinsville, Kentucky, where he was born March 18, 1877, and where he is now buried, I wandered around town talking to people who knew him, some for whom he had done readings. Was he real? Oh, yes! Down to Earth, everybody said. A good man, truly good. He taught Sunday School. He was an avid gardener. He was a good husband, father of two sons, a devout Christian. He was, absolutely everyone reported, an ordinary man.

During his lifetime he was consulted by people from every walk of life. He counseled on proper diet (which he ignored for himself), the importance of exercise, a proper attitude and above all the importance of devotion to God.

Eventually I traveled to Virginia Beach, Virginia, to the Association for Research and Enlightenment, a non-profit organization established by Cayce to further his psychic endeavors. More than fourteen thousand readings had been transcribed as he spoke. They are on file at ARE, the surest proof of his uncanny insights: predictions of things in the future, medical advice that is still referred to sixty years later by people in need.

Lying on his couch in a hypnotic trance, Mr. Cayce extracted information during "life readings" that covered a person's karma from past incarnations. People living today had lived before, some of them ten thousand years before! Some descended from Atlantis when that great continent was destroyed. Atlanteans fled to Egypt, also to present day Spain, and to the landmass that became the Americas. Out of these life readings Mr. Cayce revealed biblical history, human development, the truth about Adam and Eve, the Garden of Eden and other questions. How were the pyramids built? Has Earth been visited by beings from other planets?

In the beginning of his career as a psychic, he suffered several unhappy experiences when strangers stuck him with pins to test whether he was truly unconscious. Many wanted predictions about the stock market and tips on where to drill for oil. When he awoke from sessions like those, he suffered terrible headaches. Thereafter he insisted that his beloved wife Gertrude should act as controller, protecting him from thoughtless intrusions, senseless pricks and pinches. His secretary, Gladys Davis, came to work with Cayce September 10, 1923, and thereafter his remarks were taken down verbatim. When Cayce awoke from a trance, he usually had no idea what he had said. The transcribed readings were his only indication of what had transpired. The result was nearly fifteen thousand documented sessions delivered during his lifetime.

As his fame grew, Cayce was investigated by historians,

the medical profession, theologians, and scientists. The majority of skeptics went away convinced that Edgar Cayce was the greatest psychic who ever lived. During his lifetime he was consulted by Woodrow Wilson, George Gershwin, Irving Berlin, and Thomas Edison. But most of his readings were for the average man or woman who had a problem and needed assistance.

Many books have been written about Edgar Cayce. Thomas Sugrue's excellent biography *There Is a River* relates Cayce's early life and subsequent service to the needs of mankind. Other books described his thoughts on specific subjects, medical and physical, past and future. As a Christian, Cayce had read the Bible once for every year of his life. He was devout and prayerful. When he was a child, he had a vision of an angel who asked what he wanted to accomplish in life. Thirteen-year-old Edgar declared that he wanted to help people, particularly children. The angel indicated it would come to pass. And it did.

The more I learned about the man, the greater was my admiration. He was a good person, dedicated to worthy deeds.

So then, in early 2011, after completing my latest novel, I sat at the computer one day wondering what to write next. <u>I was astonished to see text flow onto the monitor.</u> The first sentence was exactly what you will read in the following chapters. These were not my thoughts! I'd never heard some of the words he used. "<u>Lucubration</u>," for example, <u>which means to work, write, or study laboriously, usually at night.</u>

Cayce? I called in my wife, Judith. "Look at this," I said. "I think that's Edgar Cayce!"

She gave me two aspirin and a cup of decaf coffee.

Every morning, there he was again. He woke me out of a sound sleep and I stumbled into my office and sat at the computer ready to receive.

If this was Cayce I didn't want to waste a minute of it. I began asking friends (in person and on Facebook) if they had questions they wanted to pose to him.

Most of the inquiries were mundane—will I marry next year? Will my book become a best-seller? Should I invest in the stock market again?

Cayce wouldn't reply to questions he described as "temporal." But now and then, he did answer, sometimes with humor.

Q: Why did the Mayan calendar end on December 21, 2012?

A: "The man chiseling stone got carpel tunnel syndrome and went home."

I tried not to interject myself into these messages. Maybe I succeeded and possibly I didn't, but I attempted to make the dialogue as little my own as possible.

The process was exciting and revealing. People of my acquaintance were generally forgiving of this new eccentricity, making gentle jokes about communing with Cayce. My wife, author Judith Richards, was very patient and understanding. My former wife and our writing partner, Linda Cline, encouraged me to continue. "If he could speak to the deceased when he was alive," Linda reasoned, "surely he can speak to the living now that he is dead!"

Edgar Cayce cautioned me, "Don't show off."

I hope I have been true to his wishes and that this book is something that would not embarrass him. Some days I sat for hours and nothing happened. Another time, the words poured forth. I began each session asking, "Is there anything you would like to say, Mr. Cayce?" Sometimes there was, sometimes not. As I received questions from friends and associates, online and by telephone, I relayed them immediately.

I have not rearranged the sequence of these statements, taking them down exactly as I perceived them over a period of many weeks. On occasion they were redundant. Topics would swing to the future, the past, or the present. Some of the inquiries were touching. From a mother in South Alabama came this letter on Facebook, reprinted here exactly as it was written:

> *Dear Mr. Cayce: If uR, were or visited the place we call 'heaven'—R my dogs and cats who have passed really up there fishing and having a blast w/my grandparents now? My parents told me they were. Tk u 4 this info; we miss them so much. It is of great importance to us, esp. now our daughter believes her animals R there 2. Welcome back &O! Let us know if u need a place 2 stay till U can afford a house in Baldwin County. Do U plan to live here on the coast? Good luck!*

His response is in the text that follows: "Man and beast, denizens of the sea, and birds of the firmament will share a common celestial state."

This experience has given me a new perspective on life and death and love. I come away with great affection for my fellow man.

I hope the results herein will do the same for you.

—*C. Terry Cline, Jr.*

the return of edgar cayce

"Before the body died in 1945, it said we'd be back in 2050. That alone should have told you the world would not end December 21, 2012. But now as a part of the Universal Wave that contains all of everything any of us needs, it seems important to report on what is, and what will be. Therefore these observations come from beyond the corporeal world, using the physical body of this author to take notes for your benefit.

As for the past, it has been well documented. Previous readings are at the Association for Research and Enlightenment in Virginia Beach, Virginia, United States of America. They are available for anyone to read. This is not a defense of errors in judgment, primarily because final judgment may be premature. Things that were yet to be in 1945 may have occurred unnoticed and are no less accurate, although as yet unrecognized.

There are disadvantages to entrapment in a human body. Free of physical limitations, time and space become a continuum of past, present, and future. There are no walls of daylight and dark. Years become a trillionth of a second in the tick of creation.

That which Man does not understand has always become mythic tales to explain the inexplicable. Hopefully these writings will dispel the mysticism and illuminate the truth. In the end, all that is has always been, and will forevermore be. Birth is not the onset, nor death the terminus, but merely aspects of existence. Like steam to water to solid ice, form is a visible indicator of matter. Stone can be magma crushed and molten flowing, but no less stone. The diamond is a rock. Under pressure and heat a stone becomes a gem. But it is no less a rock. Therefore we are what we are, and what we have always been. Dust and granite are not ultimate states, but phases in passing.

So it is with people, shaped by hardship, formed by personal stress; remember that heat and pressure make the jewel. Be kind in judgment of others. Life is in constant flux. Bad today becomes good tomorrow. Before you judge harshly, do not forget that what they are will change. And so will you.

Feed the hungry. Poverty is not class distinction. Penury is temporary. But also pity the rich, for that too shall pass. In the end, solid becomes vapor and over eons planets are composed of stellar dust. Nothing is permanent and everything is subject to metamorphosis.

It is a wise entity who helps those in need, because generosity ripples across the galaxy of mankind's existence and ultimately returns. Assistance extended to others is not expended, but invested. Good deeds rebound in kind. Gentle parents engender tender progeny. A compassionate hand lifts the lesser among us. Empathy is unguent for the soul, good for he who bestows sympathy as well as he who receives it.

Good devolves to those from whom good comes. Helping others we thereby help ourselves.

So now let us look at evil; should we forgive the transgressors? Would that make them better?

To pardon those who have sinned against us does not cleanse them of wickedness. A malevolent being is not purged of evil by turning the other cheek. Forgiving them, we ease the psychic strain on ourselves, because resentment is a heavy burden to bear. For a particularly heinous crime, altering evil's physical form is a sensible means of protecting ourselves. When confronted with an evil entity, convert solid to gas. Sent to another plane, the entity will have a chance to change for the better.

But do not eliminate the entity out of revenge. The purpose of converting the transgressor to a gaseous state is to protect future potential victims. If redemption is possible on the human plane, let it be so. You should forgive the offender for your own well-being, not for his.

On the plane where I now exist there is beauty no mortal could imagine. Here the universe can be traversed in an instant passing through glowing remnants of expanding heavens, into and out of the bottomless pits of imploding stars. Gravity cannot seize, nor constrain, bend or detain this spirit on intergalactic patrol. It is comfortable here. The senses do not feel heat or cold. Thermal currents can not sweep away the traveler. Plumes of solar heat do not interfere and nothing in space can destroy this spirit released from the physical bonds of the planet Earth.

In religions from every era no priest ever imagined the heaven that awaits all living things. Man and beast, denizens of the sea, and birds of the firmament will share a common celestial state. Unhindered by the need to survive and propagate, ambition does not exist. There is no hunger or deprivation.

The streets are not gold; there are no physical markers of time and place. You will not miss pleasures of the flesh. What you can expect is emotion no mortal can experience. It is intercourse without procreation, devoid of social entanglement. There are no entities here in the form of children. Spirits have no body; the desire for family is part of the lure that draws Man back to human configuration. We begin to yearn for the very things from which death has released us. It takes courage to return to a human body. The beat of a heart comes with societal, matrimonial, and psychic pressures. With birth one must begin to relearn lessons as old as mankind. Some souls do not choose to accept rebirth, but many do.

On this plane you are not one entity in the presence of another, but spirits mingling together. One does not touch in a material sense, but like liquids gently blended into a single solvent, souls conjoin. No rapture can compare. It is love in the purest form.

So therefore, fear not the passing of life for there is no death. You are coming to a place of tranquility. Priests of every faith call it heaven, and it is. But abiding in perfect harmony, there is something in the psyche of Man that seeks the challenge of discontent. In the afterbirth of a life lived long, the soul forgets the travails of being human.

Memories of hardship fade. We ache for the angst of bearing children, feeding, clothing, and educating them. As stated, that is part of the plot to entice souls back from a place of euphoria.

Fear not death. Fear life. But in all cases, remember that you are where you are because you chose to be. Don't blame God. The choice was yours.

Now then, about God.

God is what you believe God to be, because God is all things. It would be a mistake to alter Man's concept of a Supreme Being since there is no ideology that is entirely true or completely wrong. But in every case, the Deity is more than any one religion has envisioned. He is neither he nor she, this nor them, singular nor plural. He is any and all, one and many, encompassing the ever widening universe. To know the nature of God one must accept the seeming contradictions of outer space. Into black holes matter disappears, condensed to microscopic density. While at the same time, new planets are born and the universe expands.

There are laws of physics which Man does not under-stand because they are beyond human comprehension. The universe is shrinking while it expands. Antimatter is an exotic form of matter in which the electric charge of each particle is the opposite of that in normal matter. Dark matter cannot be seen, felt, tasted or measured, and yet it is the substance that holds all matter together. Gravity pulls, but also repels.

Is there a God? Yes.

Where is He? Everywhere.

You pray to Him or to them, worship one or all. The monotheist is right, there is but one god, and the mystic who prays to many gods is no less correct, for God is everything.

Does God hear you? How could it be otherwise? God is everywhere.

The concept of God is the most godly thing Man has ever done, placing a power above him, accepting a subservient position in the scheme of things. Yet even as he does so, Man tries to become God and therein is a danger to all mankind. Because in fact God is within, as well as without, a part of the particle and a piece of the flesh created as Man. The missing ingredient is wisdom that comes with maturity.

Education may be quickly acquired but sagacity is an extract of experience. Some men more than others, but no man entirely, can accumulate wisdom from schooling. From eons of experience, God has acquired infinite wisdom that is beyond the capacity of a human lifetime. Man can become wise in the span of his life and more so over many lifetimes, but a thousand lives cannot equal the profound knowledge of eternity.

In subsequent incarnations maturity and wisdom accrue. The sum total of infinite wisdom is not the path to riches or power, but realization that serving others is the ultimate enlightenment. Every entity is but a flicker of a finite flame. Before life is extinguished, the more one has given to others the closer is he to God.

So then, therefore, what awakens this entity before the self-appointed year of 2050? To reassure mankind of his survival!

It takes courage to return to human form. The last breath upon Earth was January 3, 1945. From this plane everything mundane has been observed with a detachment that comes with a distant seat overlooking the vagaries of humanity. Much has been admirable; some has been less so.

It serves no purpose to recriminate over foibles of the past. Selecting individuals to criticize reduces a complaint to a fraction of the whole. Instead, let us look upon humanity as an amalgamation of many into a single being and we will call him Man.

Ten thousand years before Christ there were one million humans on the planet Earth. It took 11,800 years to reach a billion in the year 1810. When last this entity took a breath in 1945, despite wars, famines, floods and volcanic eruptions, every person shared the world with two billion, three-hundred thousand other people.

By 2050 the population will exceed ten billion.

Within this century food and water will be in short supply. Deserts will spread as arable soil retreats. The warming of the globe will drive seashore inhabitants to higher ground. The shift of political influence from West to East will cripple existing world powers. Corporations in search of less expensive labor will swing economic centers from one region to another. Population growth will demand more space. Rain forests will be denuded. Extinction of species will escalate until it will seem only the creatures needed by humans will survive. There will be wars. Industrial nations will fight for oil and markets. Poor societies will march under ideological banners. The predominant religion will be Islamic. Instant news worldwide will leave populations depressed, convinced that the world teeters on a precipice of utter destruction. Can anyone blame this entity for his fear of returning? The world will be a mess. And yet—Man will survive.

To know what is coming we have only to examine the past. It is the natural order of things that events are circular. In that maelstrom is the surest proof of life after death: the universe contracts even as it expands. That which has been is destined to be again. It is the nature of nature to recycle. Part of regeneration is the dismantling of what has been to make way for what will be. If things were permanent, there would never be anything new. Old ways are fixed ways. Soil must be turned to be tilled. The past is beneath the feet of the present—that is why archeologists must dig to uncover ancient artifacts.

Man's memory is short. Lessons forgotten from eons past have doomed societies to national collapse. America is the greatest democracy in the history of the world. But in their day, so were Ancient Greece, Mesopotamia, and Phoenicia. Power alone will not save a nation. The decline of Rome, Spain, and England proves that riches and military dominance do not guarantee an endless existence.

External threats can be defeated. Terrorism, piracy, and ideological warfare are soon identified and abolished. The disease most likely to destroy a great nation comes from within. Its name is greed.

Owning a homestead and having control of one's environment are nesting instincts found in most species.

Territorial protection is based on the need for resources required to survive. At the end of the nineteenth century, the common desire was forty acres of soil, which was the land one man could work to support his American family. By the end of the twentieth century greed demanded more. Adequate was not enough. The avaricious entity craved land he never worked, a home larger than he needed, and possessions beyond adequate. Most creatures devote every hour to the quest for sustenance. Greedy Man strives for possession merely to possess.

The ugliness beyond hoarding is selfishness. The failure to share makes good men mean. Passing a needy entity some men tell themselves money is a bequest that is wasted on vices. What does it matter? Would you help a beggar who hoped to make payment on a house or car? Do not dictate the disposition of a gift. Leave the needy to determine his use of your donation.

The tale of the Good Samaritan has never been more relevant than today. We fear to help the helpless lest we put ourselves in peril. Do not bypass a stranded pedestrian. If you have room, share a ride. While it is true that bad things have happened to generous people, it is a rare and unfortunate consequence of helping others. Most acts of generosity are quietly and gratefully accepted by those in need.

Do not minimize the charity of rich men who give away fortunes. Whatever their motives, the charitable donation is no less beneficent. If a bequeath is given in hopes of reciprocity, it may diminish a gift in the eyes of those who give little or nothing. But the recipient is no less grateful, nor should he be. A wealthy donor should be no less admired because he could afford to give.

If you have a dollar, give a dime. If you have a dime, give a cent. If it hurts to give the gift it is all the more laudable. The end is the same: Helping meet a need is the godly thing to do. If you have no material thing to offer, give sympathy and compassion. If all else fails, give laughter. Humor is emotional currency. Be generous.

Do not be afraid to touch your fellow man. A young hand lifts an elderly heart. A hug and a kiss are transfusions for the ill and infirm. Nothing quickens the blood like the tactile brush of empathetic attendants.

Listen to the lonely. Senescence is a time of great loss: hearing, eyesight, and physical dexterity. But what the elderly miss most of all is a sense of importance. Companions no longer hear the words an old man speaks, and nobody cares what he thinks. Lean in and listen carefully. There is nothing an aging entity appreciates more than a caring ear. Look him in the eye and eschew platitudes. Respond to what he may say.

He lives in the past because there is precious little future. Ask about years gone by. He will enjoy relating remembrances. Your interest gives his history value, and indeed the elderly mind holds knowledge of things human and divine. He is eager to share, if you inquire. What does he recall from childhood? Things have changed in his lifetime—ask about them.

Know the symptoms of seniority. Tips of the fingers dry and turning a page becomes difficult. Lips benumbed by age make a kiss on the cheek more appreciated than a peck to the mouth. Fear of falling slows the motions. Muscle and bones once vibrant become doddering and feeble. But the brain awaits awakening. Youthful fantasies still abide. Distant dreams are no less vivid.

Stricken in years and decrepit in body, deep within resides the child that once marveled at tadpoles and swam naked in a pond. Awaken that youngster! Play the games he played, wade in the creeks and wander along flowered trails he knew in his youth. Help him recapture the joy of first love. If a name escapes him, it does not matter. In his ancient mind he sees faces from long ago. The scent of spring is a distant memory, but it will freshen if mentioned in conversation. So ask. And listen.

All lives encompass regret. For the unfortunate things we have done, for failure to meet the needs of others, we writhe with unhappy recollections. But it is never too late to change. We cannot undo the past, but the future is ours to mold. Waste no time bemoaning ills from long ago. Instead, take a fresh step forward and make those same errors no more. If the elderly comes to tears, let him weep. Lachrymal baths cleanse the soul and lamentation eases a guilty conscience. But then put aside those unhappy memories and go forth into a new beginning.

2050 is merely tomorrow, and that is only the rebirth. Another twenty years will mold the man that this entity hopes to become. Like all of us embarking on a new human life, memories of this existence will vanish. It is part of the plan, too. If mortal Man knew what to expect on Earth's plane, when life becomes difficult he would be tempted to end it and return to the pacific scene from which this entity speaks.

Self-annihilation ends a course without a final lesson.

There is purpose in suffering. Hardship is to life what a thickening trunk is to the tree. Torn by storms and ripped by hail, the unbowed tree is made stronger by each successive lashing. Difficulty adds fiber to character.

Happiness is a temporary respite, always appreciated, but depth of psyche does not come from serenity. Suffering is good for you.

If you are overcome by adversity, recognize it for what it is. It is your friends in the ether laminating your soul. When troubles are too much to bear, laugh it off. Thus disarmed bad luck will get better.

Let us now discuss the "friends" mentioned herein.

Greeks gave Man the word angel, which means messenger. The Bible names Gabriel and Michael, but scriptures speak of many angels. These are the spirits who attempt to guide you to what is good and right. When you pray, they are the ones who hear you and respond or not, depending on the real need of the entity. Getting what you pray for is not always best for you and this is a decision your friends make on your behalf.

Angels

The friends are with you always in dark days and sleepless nights. They stand at your side when troubled, lend strength beyond human capacity, and offer comfort to ease the anguish of loss. They make light the weight that no man can lift. Their voices are whispered intuitions that guide you around the rim of a bottomless abyss. They attend your innermost thoughts and lend counsel in sleep. Listen to those subconscious lessons.

Angles

Some thoughts are primitive, but primordial impulse helped animals survive. Suspicion kept dangerous strangers at bay. In the extreme it is racism. As populations expand and technology shrinks the globe, overcoming racial prejudice is more important than ever.

Look beyond dissimilarities of culture and seek the core that all men share. The entity with a different skin, back, and brow is your brother. Embrace him, for you are from one mother of long ago.

Man is the only animal with the intellectual capacity to rise above prejudice. It is wise to know your enemies and wiser still to know those who are no real threat at all. The rise of racism has ancient roots from days when any stranger was a possible foe. In the future it will become more important to cultivate the friendship of others.

It won't be easy to cast off distrust of the unknown. Every day, the world is exposed to the worst that mankind has to offer. Countless television programs offer detailed reports of rape, robbery, and murder. It is human nature to be captivated by stories of violence, and commercial news outlets know that. An atrocity anywhere may be broadcast everywhere within moments. The viewer is exposed to macabre tales of madness and mayhem. This has a cumulative effect and paranoia deepens. It is natural to assume the world is a treacherous place and people are not honorable.

There will always be dangers, but that is the exception and not the rule. In the end good triumphs over evil because if it did not, civilization would collapse and chaos reign. Make no mistake: it is incumbent upon honorable men to combat evil wherever they find it. But at the same time, be aware of the vast majority of people who live quiet and trustworthy lives. Assume the best until the worst is evident.

Do not live in fear of meteors that can disrupt the world. Yes, these things have happened in the past and will come again in the future, but keep your faith and live life to the fullest today. Tectonic plates collide, volcanoes erupt, and tidal waves sweep cities into the sea. Do not poison today with terrors predicted for tomorrow. Live by the words of the poet who said, 'Luck's a chance, but trouble's sure, face it as a wise man would, train for ill and not for good.'

It is prudent to lay away provisions for tomorrow. Train for ill and you will not be caught wanting. But at the same time cherish moments of peace and happiness.

There is a formula for unhappiness. It comes with sloth. Stay busy and be productive. From work, we derive satisfaction and contentment, so do not remain idle. At the same time it is useless to yearn for work you cannot accomplish. There is no good to come from illogical aspirations. We make ourselves miserable wishing for what we don't possess, almost always constructed around unrealistic desires and improbable goals. You want to write a novel, but you can't write. You'd like to be a movie star and can't act. There are a thousand things you can't do. There is one thing you can do, and it's the key to contentment.

Do for others and not for yourself. Volunteer to work a soup line and feed the needy. Join bell ringers at Christmas to help raise funds for the Salvation Army. Let charitable organizations know that you can fold pamphlets and prepare them for mailing. If you are homebound and poverty-stricken, ask what you can do for others using whatever resources are available to you. Giving of yourself will bring rewards, if you do it genuinely. To appear unselfish is not enough. You must truly be bighearted and generous.

By helping others, you are productive and busy, two necessary components of happiness. Meantime, for those unrealistic goals, master the craft and remain resolute. Learn to write. Study acting. Apply yourself to those dreams, but do it concurrently as you help others in need.

And then there is love, the perpetual quest of the human heart. We ache for the company of a caring soul, a compassionate touch, and receptive response. As years go by, love seems all the more elusive. Who could love us in years of declining youth? We lose hair, eyesight fades, and hearing slowly fails. What remains to attract adoration? Ask yourself, why are you searching for affection?

It is a common error to seek love for purely self-indulgent reasons. We all want someone to admire us, bolster our confidence, and elevate the ego. We question, what can this entity do for me? Therefore we must ask, what is love, exactly?

Love is a mutual need between two entities, a symbiotic gratification in which the voids are fulfilled in equal quantity and quality. The greater the dependence and subsequent satisfaction, the deeper emotional attachment will become. In the event of an unbalanced need in which one desires but the other does not, the resulting bond is shallow. Always look for what you can do for the other. Again, the motive must be magnanimous. Expecting nothing as recompense, ask, what need can you satisfy? Under those conditions gratitude can ripen to romance.

In pursuit of love, go forth with generous intent, and by meeting the needs of another, so then will your needs be met.

You look to the prophet for predictions of events to come, and we have dwelled upon personal matters because these attributes determine what will come. Remember this: nothing is immutable; everything is subject to change. It is within the power of the individual to determine his own fate, and collective Man has the awesome ability to shift the trajectory of history.

Now and then an individual shapes the future with inventions, political persuasion, or theocratic influence. Look at dictators like Josef Stalin and Adolf Hitler, whose reigns tragically altered the lives of millions. But then there are entities like Mahatma Gandhi who led a nation to independence.

Let us not forget Jesus Christ and Mohammad; Siddhartha Gautama, who became Buddha; Zarathustra, father of Zoroastrianism; Kong Fuzi, known as Confucius; Vardhamana, the last Jina who founded the Jain community; Laozi, whose psychology and philosophy began Taoism; Shri Guru Nanak Dev Ji, whose teachings became Sikhism; and Baha'u'llah, from whence rose the Baha'i faith.

Individuals can influence the future in lasting ways for good or for ill. Like a pebble dropped into a pond, every individual has the power to send ripples of influence to the farthest shore. It is a momentous responsibility that should not be taken lightly. Speak with care for you never know the impact of your language. Eschew words of discrimination and hatred. Do not endorse violence. The sum of individual thoughts and actions become the creed of nations.

A silent response is tacit approval and radical thoughts harden in the absence of objection. If confronted with evil, voice disapproval. A negative reaction dampens extremism. Speak up! Let it be known you are not part of a fanatical movement.

Be moderate in all things. It is the way to good health and emotional stability. Remember the readings of long ago: the key to well-being is assimilation, dissemination, and elimination. It is valid in what you eat, but also in what you absorb into the mind. Cruel words poison mental health and pollute one's outlook. The subconscious is the reservoir of all conscious input. Unkind thought becomes ulterior impulse. Purity comes from cleansed substrata of accumulated thinking.

Something dangerous is happening in the Western

world. Movies, music, television, and games expose children to graphic violence, vulgar language, and immoderate sex. Continuous scenes of degradation inure a young mind to unspeakable horrors in the same way that war hardens men in battle to death and destruction; an unemotional response that allows the soldier to maintain sanity and survive. Under the influence of entertainment media, young minds soon become accustomed to unspeakable atrocities. The result will be ever more cruel young criminals devoid of conscience even when committing abominable acts.

Treasure your language and use it judiciously. Do not insult your friends by taking God's name in vain. Do not trivialize sex with vulgar words. When enough people curse without thinking, cursing soon sounds normal. Avoid abuses of speech. Words have power to construct or destroy, enhance or disfigure; apply them as you would an indelible stain. Properly used language can beautify. Carelessly uttered words blemish and disfigure.

Treat all men as you would a child, adding strength to character with cautiously chosen comments. The seeds of self-concept are planted in susceptible minds. How we see ourselves is determined by how others see us. If a child is admired he respects himself. Through the eyes of the beholder he becomes a reflection of another person's regard. This never changes. Insults and disapproval disfigure even the hardened entity that appears to shrug it off.

Kind words are the loving strokes we bestow on others. Be generous in content and spare in offense. Speak of someone as you would have him speak of you.

If you pledge matrimonial troth, be faithful. Marriage is a sacred coupling and should not be corrupted. Resisting temptation strengthens character, so be strong in your vows. If both sides feel they received the best part of a contract, that is the test of a good agreement. If broken, the vows of wedlock are never again as strong. Make your nuptials and keep them safe from temptation; no treasure will ever be greater than the trust of a loving spouse.

Know yourself. There is no shame in weakness, nor sin in seduction, only in yielding to it. Do not put yourself in the way of temptation—for truly, the flesh is weak.

Even an ailing burro is strong pulling an empty wagon. Keep your karmic load light. A clear conscience is Man's greatest strength.

A glimpse of things to come:

By 2050, cigarette smoking will go the way of opium

dens in China. Smoking bans will spread to all the states, and the price of cigarettes will continue to rise. Counterfeiting will become a major problem in affluent societies—currency, liquor, medicine, and tobacco will be duplicated and sold as bona fide brands. The problem will become so pervasive, corporations will establish their own investigative forces and there will be assassinations to stop counterfeiting. Industrial espionage and countermeasures against it will become common.

Miniaturization will continue to reduce the size of products. Spying devices will become so small cameras and transmitters will be concealed in household products, making thefts easily traced.

Capital punishment will be abolished in Western societies, but will increase in Eastern nations as the cost of incarceration continues to increase.

The study of aberrant behavior will become more medical than punitive. In the century ahead, criminologists will specialize in pharmacology to treat convicts as patients rather than inmates. Hormonal imbalance will be blamed for many crimes.

There will be less violence in books, magazines, and movies as authors and producers become more aware of the damage those images are causing.

By the end of the twenty-first century, the influence of oil-producing nations will diminish as new inventions replace carbon fuels.

In the twenty-second century, Arabs will be trying to learn how to survive in the way of their Berber forefathers, living nomadic lives.

In the end, desert economies will collapse as former allies confiscate their holdings in the Western world. Without the power of oil politics, major producers will have little left but the sand they've lived on for centuries.

In the coming hundred years, kingdoms, monarchies, and dictatorships will be overthrown. The trend will be to theocratic governance.

Wars will become less nationalistic and more tribal. Nuclear attacks will be attempted by terrorists in America, England, France, Italy, and Germany. The result will be a massive retaliation against ideologies like Islam. But then, a response to that will be even greater faith in Muslim beliefs.

The worldwide birthrate will decline by the end of the twenty-first century as resources are stretched to their limits.

Old diseases will appear again out of jungles destroyed by developers: bubonic plague, dengue fever, and measles will become pandemic worldwide. Diseases will become immune to time-tested treatments with drugs.

Safety nets like social security systems will be diminished or abandoned outright. Elderly citizens will be treasured for their knowledge of farming, raising livestock, and preserving foodstuffs.

International distrust of governments will bring new strength to democracies. The demand for one man one vote will alter election procedures.

Education will shift from public schools to elite private institutions nurturing the brightest youths of society. All others will learn trades that will become more valuable with time: plumbing, carpentry, and mechanical repairs. The emphasis will be on maintenance designed to make things last longer.

By the year 2150, wealth will be judged by personal happiness and contentment, not material possessions.

The right-to-die movement will gain prominence, with assisted suicide deemed an acceptable alternative to suffering.

The emphasis on long life will give way to good life as attitudes change about extending the earthly existence of the terminally ill.

A common theme will become, 'There is a time to die.'

Medical facilities will be feared as a source of fatal diseases such as staph.

Ancient belief in reincarnation will prevail.

Through it all, Man will survive.

This reading is ended for now."

"In the year 2210, interplanetary discoveries will introduce Earth to life-forms on other planets. Thousands of other worlds will be recognized. The immense distance across the galaxies will prohibit invasions by one world against another. Communication between worlds will come centuries before Earthman sets foot on the turf of another species of humans. The deliberate transfer of DNA from one world to another will take place in a spacecraft that requires hundreds of years to complete the journey between worlds.

Faith in God will be strengthened by DNA evidence proving that humans living on countless planets are related and all spring from a single source.

Ready for questions."

Q: From the perspective of the Universal Wave, how does the world appear to you?

A: "The same way the world appears to you if considering a period in the distant past. How do you see the year 1000, for example? The past from a perspective of several hundred years gives a viewer a philosophical attitude about many events that seemed critical at the time."

Q: When will the world end?
A: "Read the Bible. Nobody knows the answer to that question."

Q: Why does the Mayan calendar end December 21, 2012?
A: "The Mayan calendar ends December 21, 2012, because the fellow chiseling the rock got carpal tunnel syndrome and went home."

Q: In your readings prior to January, 1945, did you predict the end of the world?
A: "No."

Q: Was Nostradamus for real?
A: "Yes."

Q: How is it possible to tell the future?
A: "Anyone can predict the future by recognizing trends and mathematical probabilities. Everything in the future can be influenced by the will of Man. As herein stated,

one man can alter the future; all mankind can alter the future mightily."

Q: What can an individual do to make mankind better?
A: "Help those who need assistance. Live not for yourself, but for others as well."

Q: What is the longest time a man has lived?"
A: "According to the Bible, Methuselah, the son of Enoch, lived 969 years. Peng Zu of China lived 800 years in the Yin Dynasty. Abdul Azziz Al-Hafeed Al-Habashi lived 674 years. Saint Servatius the bishop of Tongeren was 375 years old when he died in May, 384. Devraha Baba, an Indian Siddi Yoga saint, died in 1989 after living 700 years."

Q: Is it possible to live that long nowadays?
A: "Anything is possible. Take care of yourself."

Q: Why are you coming back to Earth in 2050?"
A: "Hopefully to reassure mankind.

   This reading is ended for now."

"A new form of propulsion will be discovered before the end of the twenty-third century. Driven by dry fuel of unlimited duration, rockets will map the planets and radio information to earthbound scientists. Robots will do the exploring.

On Earth, labor-saving devices will assume the form of built-in appliances that talk to you, a boon for lonely people. Time will be regulated by the decay of radioactive materials and satellite clocks will regulate the world's timepieces.

Wood will cease to be the main building material, giving way to polymers and metals. Metallurgical breakthroughs will produce lighter, stronger, cheaper skeletons for structures.

Cremation will replace most burial practices as the cost of funerals becomes prohibitive, and space more precious.

Federal income tax evasion will force governments to establish value-added collections in which a fee is included at the point of manufacturing.

In an effort to save water, laundry soap will be replaced by molecular agitation systems that clean clothes electronically.

In the year 2135, landfills will be mined for waste that can be recycled. Trash in private homes will be recycled on the premises and used to generate heat and air conditioning.

In 2345 this entity will return once again to reassure mankind.

By 2300 in most civilized nations, newborn babies will be routinely tagged for DNA identification, thereby making it more difficult for criminals to avoid detection.

The trend to plastic instead of paper currency will continue. Bank accounts will be established at birth for lifelong service to the consumer.

2250: Public transportation will be reinstated nationally in America as the price of petroleum products continues to climb. High speed railway systems will span the world.

2225: Insurance will become a government function, replacing policies underwritten by private corporations against windstorm, flood, and other natural disasters.

2200: The publication of books, magazines, and newspapers will be completely replaced by electronic duplication delivered to consumers on handheld viewers.

2450: After several nuclear accidents around the world, consumers will turn to a form of Tesla coils to generate power for individual homes. The wireless transmission Tesla system will bring a new appreciation for Nikola Tesla, the Serbian-born inventor, mechanical engineer, and electrical engineer.

I will not be born knowing who I am; that is not part of the plan. The discovery of identity will come when exposed to readings that begin to sound true and normal. That may occur as early as 2070 depending on this entity's parental influences.

As has been stated in the previous incarnation: the magnification of any desire which seeks only selfish gratification must eventually bring upon its creator anguish and final destruction. God created woman by dividing the spiritual being of Man, thus creating a spiritual balance and preparing the way for a conquest of good over evil.

In 1968 the extinct continent of Atlantis was rediscovered by James W. Mavor, Jr., an American with the

Woods Hole Oceanographic Institution. An intact city of two- and three-story houses still stands under ash of the volcanic explosion that sank the city. Frescoes are beautifully preserved. The absence of skeletons and gold indicates a massive evacuation by the residents prior to the destruction. This is not the entirety of Atlantis and should not be construed as the total picture but only a part of it. After the first destruction of a single continent, there remained five large islands and that is the totality of Atlantis.

In eons past, the surface of the world was different than it is now. The axis of the Earth has changed since then. Polar regions were tropical. The Nile emptied into the Atlantic Ocean. The Sahara Desert was inhabited and fertile. In America the Mississippi basin was under the ocean.

In the beginning before Man was material he was spirit without body, as am I now in the Universal Wave. He could project himself in any direction he desired. The flaw in Man was his desire for sensory pleasures, and all too often he strove toward that end. It is this weakness that pulls mankind into mind-bending addictions trying to alter reality with sensory titillations like liquor and narcotics.

Many soul entities became obsessed with carnal gratification. The quest for those sensations is one of the things that lure Man back into physical Earth form. Thus sex came into the world, not for procreation, but for pleasure.

The world is being greatly influenced even today by Atlanteans. Recent rapid scientific advances are evidence of their influence. Great discoveries yet ahead will come from their potency. These souls reincarnated from Atlantis will bring rockets powered by forces from the sun's rays, which are caught and reflected by crystals. There is not one leader of any nation, good or bad, who is not descended from Atlantis.

Be faithful to that which is committed to your safekeeping. Life is precious because it is of the Maker and the beginning. Learn lessons from that which is around you, whispering wind in the trees, laughter of children at play, and the pleasing sigh of contented loved ones. Within you is a spark of the molecule that was your creator. Nurture and covet it. Let goodness shine from within and allow others to bask in the radiance of your presence.

Remember the promise: If ye will be my children, I will be thy God. When ye turn your face from me, my face is turned from thee.

What can one person do when it seems all the rest of the world does nothing to improve the lot of mankind?

Care for those of lesser means. Share your good fortune with the depressed and downtrodden.

The greatest accomplishment of any entity is to be loved by a child. Properly nurtured, the love of a child will last forever. Cultivate the respect of children and they will be friends for a lifetime.

To conquer the world, first conquer yourself. That war won, the rest will come naturally.

It was not given to Man to know the time of the end of the world for fear he would be obsessed by that knowledge at the expense of the present. Knowing about lives he has lived causes Man to dwell on the past, therefore that cognizance is denied to him.

Know this above all else: Man will survive. Be then therefore as one with your maker. Love your friends and family. It is the way to enlightenment.

This reading is finished for now."

"The expectation of the rising of Atlantis has been misconstrued. Man today expected a single site to appear. In fact Atlantis, or Poseidian, was many places, as Europe is many places, or the Americas are many places. Atlantis was five locations. Look not for a single upheaval. As predicted, Atlantis arose in 1968.

You are an atom, a corpuscle in the body of God, thus a co-creator with Him in what you think and what you do. You change every soul you meet, literally or mentally. Hence, be aware of how you treat others. Your imprint is upon them. At the same time, every soul also affects you. Choose your associates carefully."

Q: What do you say to a person who does not believe in God?

A: "Doubt is a natural part of maturation. With maturity comes assurance and confidence. One does not have to believe in God to know there's life after death, for example. It is the natural order of things to recycle. As stated herein, the universe contracts and expands at one and the same time."

Q: How many worlds sustain life as Earthmen know it?
A: "If the answer were six or ten or twelve, you would comprehend and believe. There are billions of galaxies with solar systems similar to Earth's."

Q: Is each of those worlds similar to Earth's biosphere?
A: "In some cases they are souls without material bodies. The inhabitants of each world are adapted to their environments. But throughout the universe each soul has been fashioned in the likeness of the Creator. Whatever their differences in form, their lessons are basically the same: live to serve others, seek peace and not strife."

Q: Through past readings you indicated that Jesus Christ had been on Earth many times in various incarnations and each of those spiritual entities was here to serve particular peoples. Is that correct?
A: "The prophets are as one with rare exceptions. The approach may be different, but the message is fundamentally the same. You are here as this entity by choice. Make

the most of it. Do as has been herein stated.

   This reading is finished for the moment."

Q: One more question, please, sir. Sir? Sir—

(The next day Mr. Cayce began):

"Time and space have no relevance in the Universal Wave. On Earth, Man encumbers himself with an artificial index of age. In societies where age is not counted by years, Man remains youthful until the spirit vacates the body. In those societies, the only accurate index is accomplishment. An infant crawls, and then he walks; he soon runs, he masters skills of adolescence, and finally attains manhood. Thereafter the passing years are important only insofar as his skills are concerned.

In a similar manner, a man's ability is too often tied to artificial indexes society has placed upon him. He's very smart for his age, a teacher might say. He is still a good athlete in spite of his years. He's very sharp for a man so old.

A child aspires to be old, and then for the rest of his

life struggles to stay young. Do not instill pride or mortification based on the number of days an entity has existed in human form. In fact, souls who live many lives are hundreds, or thousands of years old. To say a soul is six, ten, twenty, forty, or seventy is misguided. You could just as well say he's two thousand, six thousand, or ten thousand years old.

The truest rule by which to judge a person is not age, but seasoning. Some old souls bring forward lessons from prior incarnations and they are born wise. When they have learned all that this plane has to teach, coming back to a human existence is a boring waste of time. Thereafter they usually go to a higher plane."

Q: Is there any one religion that most nearly attains the level of understanding that you have espoused?
A: "Certain swamis schooled in the ancient Vedic scriptures know these things: when their purpose on the planet Earth has been fulfilled, they have the ability to close their eyes and abandon the human body at will. Their form of worship makes them at home in a Christian cathedral, Jewish synagogue, Greek temple, Chinese pagoda, Hindu temple, Islamic mosque, Buddhist stupa, Egyptian temple, or Shinto shrine. They believe in the fundamental

truths taught by all the great bibles of the world. They adhere to the precepts of the Rig-Veda that 'Truth is One (although) men call it by various names.'

They accept all saviors and prophets, and honor all saints. The accent is on love and service, sympathy and inclusiveness. All races and nations, creeds and religions find a place within their fold.

This does not mean an entity should forsake his own religion and go to the Rig-Veda instead. Rather, the entity should endeavor to lift his religion to a comparable state.

Good mannerisms defeat bad customs, therefore practice good habits and the bad will be displaced. It is easy to slip into sloppy behavior and difficult to extricate yourself thereafter. Hence, begin early to commit the sub-conscious to worthwhile pursuits. Attitudinize posture and beware of affected poses. Present yourself humbly and suppress pretensions with a modest demeanor.

Every entity has powers he himself does not always realize. It is possible to defy gravity when under stress. Feats of incredible strength have been documented by entities under pressure. Part of this comes from one's friends who may materialize at critical times in an entity's life. Thus, survivors of life-threatening situations claim someone, or something, appeared to guide them out of danger. It was the friends, the so-called guardian angels, who stepped in to give the entity strength and resolve. Sometimes they see these friends, other times they merely sense them. Those friends are always available to you when needed."

Q: What is the key to attaining a happy marriage?
A: "As already stated herein, caring one for the other in equal degrees of intensity builds romance. Mutual need determines the depth of love. Marriage should be an extension of courtship. Romance should not end with marriage. Being cognizant of the needs of the spouse, and always vigilant in answering to those needs, happiness will be an everyday aspect of the coupling."

Q: Will there ever be world peace?
A: "As foretold by the King James Bible, yes, for a thousand years after the Second Coming."

Q: Is there really an Antichrist?
A: "Yes."

Q: What form will the Antichrist take?
A: "The fruits of the spirit of the Christ are love, joy, obedience, long-suffering, brotherly affection and kindness. Consequently, the spirit of the Antichrist is hate,

contention, strife, fault-finding, lovers of self, lovers of praise. These spirits of the Antichrist take possession of groups, masses, and show themselves in the lives of men."

Q: What is hell?
A: "Hell is of your own construction. It is what you have built for yourself. You and you alone set limits of the hell you will endure.

We are through for now."

Q: Will all the world's religions ever come together as one religion?

A: "In the beginning, Man entered the Earth plane as unattached spirits; individuals were more thought forms than individual personalities as seen today. It was Man who fashioned the human bodies which they now occupy. Hoping to discover the best form with which to experience all the sensations available to the entity, they experimented with many shapes. From tiny bodies to giants that were ten to twelve feet tall and well-proportioned throughout, the spirits tried them on. In the early period there were both giants and pygmies, monstrosities from the mixing of the thought forms. As thoughts, the spirits sought a suitable configuration for earthly existence and thus the human shape was eventually perfected in the body of Adam.

Gradually, the laws of heredity and environment took hold. In the days of Atlantis before the great destruction, the Atlanteans were a people of extremes. Some were perfect in form with appealing features; others were afflicted with hideous bodies.

All souls in the beginning were One with the Creator. That was the only time when religions were one as you speak of it. Man invented the rituals and taboos of various religions, usually for the aggrandizement of Man himself. In fact, except rarely, all religions are one today. It is the practice and rituals of religions that differ. These things we have stated repeatedly.

Eventually the five races of Man will blend as one. There will no longer be red, white, black, brown, and yellow, but a melding of them into beautiful and perfect humanity. This will take millennia, but it will occur in time. At that point, with renewed appreciation of harmony and unity, in conjunction with discovery of life on other worlds, all mankind will begin to see religion in more compatible terms. This will begin to happen in the year 3300 and will develop thereafter.

Prognosticating comes with a caveat. Virtually everything can be changed by a sum total of like minds. If Man learns to put aside hatred and overcome enmity, he will be on the threshold of universal awareness. This is what the Creator has always wanted. Toward this end, Man is making progress even now. Mankind is maturing and will continue to do so."

Q: Will war ever be outlawed?
A: "It is outlawed now. Already powerful nations have stepped in to tribal disputes to end a threat of genocide. This became law with the Nuremburg trials of Nazi criminals in the late '40s. There will always be internecine battles between families of Man. To prevent the spread of those quarrels a strong government must be ready to intercede. For now that is the United States. It will eventually become Russia and China."

Q: Will there ever be an international government?
A: "It is already taking shape with currency in common, such as the euro. Collapse of the American dollar and rampant counterfeiting will bring about banking laws that will dictate forms of government. That is tantamount to international control."

Q: What about North Korea's leader, Kim Jong-il?
A: "What about him in what regard?"

Q: Will he be a threat to world peace?
A: "No. He will leave the Earth plane soon. His young-
est son, Kim Jong-un, will take over the government of
North Korea and move toward peaceful relations with his
neighbors. Other nations will thwart plots to assassinate
the new leader. Kim Jong-un will lead his nation to prosperity and peaceful coexistence."

Q: Who will be the American president when you come
back in 2050?
A: "There are too many variables to make an accurate
prediction. A new political party is forming; old alliances
are changing. The best prospects are names you do not
know because they are too young at this time. The American public is losing faith in their elected officials. This is
a common sequence of events with declining societies.
Representatives become self-serving with exorbitant per-
quisites. Public discontent will alter many careers.

For the moment this consultation is finished."

Q: With wars and diseases killing so many people, what is the value of one life?

A: "Every entity is a microcosm of the whole. A single molecule is a study of the universe in miniature. A grain of sand is indicative of the beach. Each life is a part of the Creator. The Creator does not look upon the mass that is humanity, but rather the individual of whom the mass is comprised. Life is a manifestation of God, therefore the value of one life is great."

Q: What do you expect to find when you return?

A: "The world will be the old world yet, people will be intrinsically the same. There will always be interest in what the future may hold; toward that end this entity hopes to be of value. But remember, rebirth of the body human does not bring with it a memory of this incarnation. That must be learned anew, with each new borning. For this entity knowledge of self will come in subsequent years following discoveries of past lives and readings such as this."

Q: Will you be able to reveal future events upon your return?
A: "It has been said so."

Q: Do you equate yourself with Christ and the other prophets?
A: "Absolutely not. The prophets of which you speak brought messages from God. I am devout, but not divine."

Q: You have said that Islam will be the major religion. Does that mean Christianity will be less important?
A: "Not at all. Presently, Christianity is the largest religion in the world. That includes Catholic, Protestant, Eastern Orthodox, Pentecostal, Anglican, and many others. At the time of this reading, Christianity comprises 33 percent and Islam 21 percent of the world's religions. Islam will become predominant by weight of numbers. Then it will begin to lose adherents in the next two hundred years."

Q: Was Mohammed a true prophet?

A: "Yes."

Q: Was Christ the Son of God?
A: "As has been stated repeatedly, all mankind is the progeny of God."

Q: Have extraterrestrials ever visited Earth, and will they return?
A: "You are them and here you are."

Q: Are tragedies punishment from God?
A: "No."

Q: Survivors often attribute their survival to God. Is that justified?
A: "Yes, in that many times it is their friends who see them through. But the friends do not deliberately inflict suffering upon the entities."

Q: Please name the greatest prophets to have served mankind.
A: "Early prophets included Hosea, Joel and Amos. Isaiah, Jeremiah, and Ezekiel are Major Prophets along with Moses and Noah. Then there's Daniel in the English Bible. Twelve Minor Prophets are named in the Greek Twelve Prophets book Dodecapropheton. Consider also oral

prophets who left no record of their teachings, including Jahaziel, Huldah, Ahijah, Elijah, Jahu, Oded, Shermaiah, Azariah, and Hanani. Read 1 Samuel and 2 Samuel. As it is understood in the present plane, the word 'prophet' means an authorized spokesman for God. To name them all would take hours. Many have come and gone on to other planes with little notice except locally."

Q: Where was the Garden of Eden?
A: "This was not a walled space with a clearly defined gate. It covered an area in southeastern Turkey near the present town of Urfa. Wildlife was abundant, food easy to acquire. Archaeologists have discovered Gobekli tepe where early Man overlooked a land rich with all they desired. The failings of human nature, including boredom and waste, ended the cornucopia referred to as Eden."

Q: As a result, Man became mortal and must die?
A: "Death in the context that those previous incarnations will not be remembered, yes. But in fact spirit souls do not die."

Q: In the study of 14,000 readings you gave prior to January 3, 1945, you gave advice on buying stocks, drilling for oil, finding proof of ancient civilizations, as well

as health problems. Is that what you intend to do upon your return to this plane?

A: "Helping commercial interests with selfish motivations was a mistake. Hopefully that will not happen again. From this plane looking back over that incarnation, reaching the Universal Wave should not be trivialized."

Q: After your earthly demise, did you meet God?"

A: "At sunrise you gaze into the golden eye of God, and in the peaceful shroud of dusk you hear the nocturnal beat of His celestial heart. Not a minute passes when you are not near to God if you wish to be. Death of the body releases the spirit to a freedom that spans the universe. The encounter of which you speak is with the friends who have stood by your incarnation. To be closer to God takes more than one incarnation."

Q: Does that mean we have no chance of actually meeting God?

A: "If meeting God is the goal, you must strive for spiritual perfection. Devote your life to doing good things."

Q: In the Bible, people who devoutly believed in God suffered inordinately. According to the scriptures, God punished Man with terrible afflictions. What kind of

God is that?

A: "Plagues, pestilence, floods, famines, and earthquakes are not caused by God. Those are normal cycles of natural phenomena. To explain them, Man says that God moves in mysterious ways. That is a roundabout way of blaming God because He did not stop misfortunes. God has set in motion the ongoing cycles of nature. He has sent your friends to help you, but it is beyond the power of your friends to avert calamities of global proportion. All they can do is help you cope with danger. Do not fault God for natural disasters."

Q: Are you positive that what you say is correct?

A: "The Universal Wave is available to anyone if they will but listen. Traveling the galaxies in spirit comes after the entity is free of the body human. If earthly Man will pause and reflect, he will hear the voices of infinity. Those who practice meditation are most likely to contact the spirits with oversights of the past, present, and future."

Q: Are our deceased loved ones truly with us, or do we only imagine that?

A: "If you wish to be in the presence of a person on another plane, make yourself receptive with quiet intro-spection. Visualize the human form of the spirit you wish to be with. Imagine the features as you remember them, the contours of face and body. Don't hurry. The entity you seek may be billions of light years away and busy with other thoughts. Concentrate. Do you see the eyes and brow, the lips and chin, the body as it was in the last earthly incarnation? Bask in the presence of your loved one. Upon the death of someone dear to you, for a period of time the deceased entity is with you constantly. Eventually, the images begin to fade. Do not be distressed. That means the spirit has found the way and is off and about. The sorrow you feel is for self, not the spirit who passed to another plane. Do not begrudge the transition. Be happy for them. Be happy for yourself. Go on with life."

Q: I am afraid of dying. Is there anything you can offer that will ease my fears?

A: "When you are weary after a long hard day, do you dread sleep? In a truly restful sleep you are free of pain and worry. Upon awakening, have you ever wished to slumber longer? How wonderful it is when you can do so, slipping back into the unconscious. That is how you will welcome the end of earthly life. Lay down your head fearlessly and succumb to sleep. The arms of Morpheus will deliver you into the magnificent reveries of eternity."

Q: Can you define what is good, and what is evil?"
A: "There is no such thing as good or evil. What many define as 'evil' can be forgiven. What many define as 'good' can devolve into something despicable."

Q: Does that mean there is no hell?
A: "As has been stated, hell is created by the entity. He alone will endure the punishment of his own making.

Do not trivialize the project at hand with temporal inquiries. If this subject cannot be treated seriously, perhaps you are the wrong one to transcribe these dictations. To minimize the readings is to suggest a lack of faith in them. If you harbor doubts about the veracity of these readings, you cannot produce notes faithfully. You apologize to this entity for doubting the source of insights, suggesting skepticism as to the universal connection between us. Answer me, please."

(**My rejoinder**): Mr. Cayce, forgive me for occasional disbelief in what has been revealed here. Admittedly, if these thoughts are not yours, to whom do they belong? Certainly not me. I don't remember ever thinking about these topics before. When I go to reference sources to check spelling and facts, again and again all you've said is true. But how do I convince myself that these thoughts are not from my own subconscious mind?

(**He said**): "Perhaps you need to step back and meditate on all that is happening here. Seek the truth through contemplative lucubration. When you have decided what you want to do, call for me again."

(**I said**): Please don't leave. Let's go on with the work. Do you have anything you'd like to say at this time?

(**He said**): "As concerns public celebrations over the death of Osama Bin Laden, be not of good cheer for the passing of any entity.

Admittedly to the Western world this entity was a fearsome terrorist. Nevertheless, his passing from the earthly plane should be regarded soberly and without merrymaking. Your worst enemy in this incarnation may be your best friend in the next. Or vice versa, a good companion this time may be a destructive force in subsequent associations. As heretofore stated, judge others kindly, for that which is today may be reversed tomorrow."

Q: May I impose upon you for a personal question regarding myself?

A: "No. That is not the purpose of what we do here together."

(I asked anyway.)

Q: Years ago I had extrasensory perception. My father was facing open heart surgery and he was afraid. He asked me if I thought he'd survive the surgery. I looked within and saw nothing unsettling. I assured my father he'd be all right. He died after the operation when an orderly placed a mask over his face to put moisture in his lungs. It was supposed to have been there for ten minutes. The orderly forgot it and as a result my father drowned. If ESP serves no purpose to me when it's important, I wanted nothing else to do with it. This is my first venture into the metaphysical since then. Please explain to me how I missed the signals of impending death of a man I loved so much.

A: "Your father asked if the surgery was a threat to his life. You answered truthfully. His death was the result of a careless attendant's inattention to duty. Your ESP did not fail you.

This reading is over for now."

"A drop of ocean water is a miniature ocean with all the radiations of such a body. As heretofore stated, a single atom is the universe in miniature. A microscopic cell is a mirror image of the macrocosm."

Q: When we dream about departed loved ones, are we actually with them, or is it a figment of our imagination?"
A: "Love goes far beyond the grave. You are with them.

You should not try to contact a deceased loved one with hopes of acquiring universal information. The entity that has passed on does not acquire greater knowledge, but knows only that which he knew when he died. Most have no more knowledge in the spiritual plane than they had on Earth. If God sends a messenger, accept him, and heed the message. But direct intercession by the Creator is not likely."

Q: What about abortion?

A: "Fetal abortion is an abomination in the eyes of most religions. The subject, however, demands a closer examination. The legal ramifications can be addressed only by laws extant in areas where the abortion is scheduled to take place. Laws vary from one locale to another. Medically, abortion is the purview of the doctor who comes to the subject with sonograms, blood tests, and internal imagery. He is in the best position to judge the necessity for an abortion. Many things can go wrong in a pregnancy and thereby termination of pregnancy may be essential for the health and well-being of the mother. Then, there are the moral issues, quite apart from legal and medical considerations. Even this is not set in stone. Morality is determined by mores of the community and may vary widely from one society to another. In the final analysis, judgment of abortion falls to the mother, who must make the decision to give up a fetus. Whatever the outcome, God understands."

Q: What about gay marriage?

A: "Again the answers lie in the tripartite response given for abortion: legal, medical, and moral. The coupling of same-sex individuals has a long history that has been well documented; all the way back beyond Alexander the Great and his male lover, Hephaestion. Alexander's father, Philip II, pursued young male lovers all his life. Philip died at the hands of Pausanias, a jealous former lover thrown over for a prettier young boy. Aristotle had a few loving men in his life, too. Such couplings were frowned upon by some ancient societies for fear it vitiated masculinity and threatened the empires. Other societies accepted and appreciated homosexual love affairs. Such liaisons ebb and flow with temperament of the times. That which is today will not be tomorrow; attitudes change. In a Biblical sense, marriage was designed for male and female with the purpose of creating children. Marriage protected the woman and her children legally and emotionally. It is not for this entity to pass judgment on temporal subjects."

Q: How would you describe yourself to a fifteen-year-old boy who never heard your name before?
A: "This entity is the harmony of body, mind, and soul, whose purpose is to help others. He is a man who cares about mankind."

Q: Should stem cell research be allowed to continue?
A: "Yes, with strict controls. Destruction of one life (fetus) to extend another life is tantamount to murder.

Harvesting fetal tissue must be done with reverent care. Faith is the bridge that spans the gulf between the seen and the unseen. Incarnations and reincarnations continue to repeat; the existence of the entity is evermore. However, terminating what might become life is not the same as terminating a life in full bloom. By 2170, duplicating human cells will be mastered and the question becomes moot."

Q: More and more young men grow up with no role models, listening to vile rap music. Will that continue?
A: "This too shall pass."

Q: Is it all right to divorce a spouse?
A: "It depends on the reason for divorce. Every step in human relations should be forward. If the end result of divorce means more productive and happy entities, then severance is good. Marriage must serve each entity well; otherwise parting company may be best. As stated before, love is a matter of reciprocity. One cannot love that which does not love in return. To love that which does not love you is not love; at best it is admiration, at worst it is obsession.

In all cases, strive for reunification whenever possible. Relationships fail for a variety of reasons. One entity is not giving equally to the other. Either or both parties grow out of the relationship as one matures and the other does not. Sometimes outside forces come to bear, such as acute distress over finances, or emotional devastation over the death of a child.

Talk to your partner. Try to remember what made you fall in love. Recall happy moments together when the two of you worked and lived as one. If all efforts fail to reignite emotions of times past, go your separate ways amicably. Do not be greedy in the division of properties. Be generous in the sharing of youthful hearts; do not punish children with pettiness between adults. Try to be friends, or at least be friendly."

Q: Will there be another prophet of Edgar Cayce's abilities between now and the year 2050?
A: "There are three currents of man: conscious, subconscious, and super conscious. The entity that is Nostradamus was an astronomer, clairvoyant, palmist and seer. He was reborn and known once as Sybil and then as Isaiah. His spirit is now known collectively as Extrasensory Perception. His spirit is one of the many this entity has called upon from time to time.

There have been and will continue to be prophets,

mystics, and seers to one degree or another. Not all will use their insights in the same manner. Some will devote their abilities to solving crimes for the police. Another will seek lost articles or missing persons. Yet another will learn parlor tricks to amuse friends.

Extrasensory perception is not limited to prognostication. Many mothers experience a sense of discovery—or loss—where their children are concerned. Love comes with a burden of fear and evinces itself in times of great importance, or stress. There have been many cases where a mother sat upright in bed at night and realized a loved one had just perished on a foreign battlefield.

These talents of which you inquire are available to everyone if the entities choose to develop them. Fair warning, it is not a blessing to know when someone will die or suffer financial failure. Knowledge of future events places a heavy responsibility on the psychic. It is a burden he bears alone, and not always happily. What advantage comes from knowing the date and hour of imminent demise? All entities will leave the Earth plane eventually. Knowing the point of departure does not benefit any psychic. The clairvoyant who sees the hour and cause of physical death must shelter the thought and share it not. The revelation may be detrimental.

During World War II the president of the United States, Franklin Delano Roosevelt was informed of his impending death. He had requested the information because as president during wartime there were things he needed to do before dying. The psychic Jeane Dixon related the truth regretfully. Knowing the president would soon die was an onerous weight to carry and she could not share the information with anyone. There is no pleasure in knowing such a thing ahead of the event.

Prescience is often called a curse by those who possess insights into the future. Most psychics also say that the ability does not serve them at all. When this entity existed in human Earth form, trying to use these insights for selfish personal reasons rarely produced positive results. There were times when predicting coming events for self created terrible headaches and nausea. Overworking psychic insights drains the body human of vital life forces. Trying to respond to desperately worried inquisitors about the safety of loved ones during the war, hundreds of pleas overburdened self. The result was strokes, weakness, and death January 3, 1945.

Do not hope to acquire precognition for selfish purposes. If the ability comes upon you, use it for the benefit of others, not self. Purity of motive is the only protection

the seer has against self-destruction from overextending
the mind and body."

**Q: Do you regret anything about your life stay on Earth
from birth March 18, 1877, to death on Earth January 3,
1945?**

A: "Many things are regretted, for that is the nature of
human life and sensitivity. This entity wishes he had
devoted more time to family needs. Loving someone
means you sacrifice for them. Upon the time of dying
it was asked of his beloved, what did I sacrifice for you?
Not enough. The entity's work always came first and fore-
most. Is there not ego in such endeavors?

There is regret also that the body was taxed and
depleted by overwork during the days of war when hundreds of inquiring minds wanted to know about loved
ones. It would have been wise to marshal strength and
limit readings to two a day as had been instructed. The
entity had been warned to get rest for inner strength.
Readings drained away life resources drastically.

There are regrets also for vain attempts to make
money, to further the building of a hospital, and to make
life easier for the family.

Regrets for time wasted in trivial pursuits.

Regrets for prayers not rendered or lazily made brief, thereby shirking reverence to God, for He needs much reassurance from his creations. Prayers delivered hastily are shallow. This entity wishes he had concentrated more diligently on prayerful thanks for the many blessings bestowed upon him.

There are hundreds, perhaps thousands of petty regrets for short-tempered reactions toward persons closest to self. Impatience is a self-absorbed way of belittling the requirements of others.

Yes. Many regrets."

Q: Were you ever tempted by any woman other than your wife?
A: "No gentleman would answer such a question. It serves no purpose. By way of clarification, know this: there was no love like the love self had for wife, Gertrude. She made possible all the good things of the earthly sojourn.

This meeting is ended for now."

"Before the end of the twenty-first century, all felons will be typed for their DNA. Also, newborn babies will be typed for DNA. Despite protests concerning privacy invasions, the practice will extend from Europe, where it began, to most of the world. By 2120 new babies will be issued DNA identification cards. Missing persons will be readily identified, as well as unidentifiable bodies from battlefields. Many crimes will be quickly solved with DNA evidence from the lifetime markers.

Life in civilized nations will become more and more transparent as corporations and governments follow the purchasing habits of consumers. Video film rental histories can already predict with great accuracy what movies a person will enjoy. Large retailers can peg the likes and dislikes of customers based on their history of purchasing products. Telemarketing will become more accurate as the body of data builds, all of it tied to the DNA of the individual."

Q: In a reading from June 12, 1926, you mentioned information about the sphinx that would someday be found in the forearm, or leg, of the prostrate sphinx. Is it still there?

A: "It is and will remain so until the existence of Man is ready to receive it."

Q: The information is in a room beneath the right paw?

A: "In the base of the leg, in a cornerstone, as reported in the 1926 reading."

Q: These records are about what?

A: "The evolution and eventual destruction of Atlantis, also the building of the great pyramids and the sphinx. As yet undiscovered is a hall between the sphinx and a chamber of records, which will reveal all at a time when Man is ready to receive it."

Q: That time is not yet?

A: "Apparently."

Q: What will be the relevance of the information when it is finally revealed?

A: "There will be a new awakening in many parts of the world."

Q: Please be specific; where are those records located?
A: "In the tomb of records, a part of the Hall of Records which has not yet been uncovered. It lies between, or along, that entrance from the Sphinx to the temple—or the pyramid; in a pyramid of its own."

Q: When will they be uncovered?
A: "As stated before, when Man is ready to receive them. Remember that most things are wrought on the anvil of public opinion. If sufficient entities affect an incident, the timing will change.

We are through for now."

Q: Is the United States presence in the Middle East only about oil?

A: "For the most part, yes. Oil is vital to the American economy. Protecting the source is important. The USA is unlikely to rush into combat in places where humanitarian considerations are uppermost.

They should not be faulted for this. No nation can afford to be everywhere. Like any wise combatant, America must choose its battles carefully."

Q: Will the U.S. go back to drilling for oil in our own territories any time soon?

A: "They have never stopped."

Q: If there will be an Antichrist, will he also have come from Atlantis?

A: "More than likely he will be a descended Atlantean."

Q: Will Israel survive?

A: "Yes, for the foreseeable future."

Q: Will Man's extreme divisions lessen over time? Will we become more tolerant of others?

A: "As it has already been given herein, yes."

Q: Why do governments suppress new technology?

A: "What makes you think they do? In fact, it is far more likely that new advances will be seized for military purposes rather than be ignored."

Q: What is causing the huge and rapid rise of autism? Is it only in America, or is it worldwide?

A: "Autism and Asperger's syndrome are similar afflictions. Both have been around for many centuries but were not diagnosed as what they were. The cause in both cases stems from a genetic disposition caused by chemicals absorbed by the bodies of the parents, principally the mother. Eventually, researchers will isolate the cells that cause these problems, and they will learn to control them. They are close to that now, using various drugs to calm the one and augment the other."

Q: Is Alzheimer's a disease?

A: "It is not a disease in the sense that it stems from exposure to a virus. Alzheimer's is presenile dementia with hyaline degeneration of the smaller blood vessels in the brain generally thought to be caused by faulty metabolism and misguided nutrition. Mental deterioration occurs as the blood vessels are impeded. Onset can be delayed with proper exercise, careful planning of diet, and medicines that increase blood flow to the brain. There is a genetic disposition to the dementia. If any family member has Alzheimer's, it indicates others may be subject to the same sad fate. The symptoms may be brought on by medical intoxication, chronic infection, anemia, severe depression, stroke, brain tumor, vitamin deficiency, or thyroid disease. Alzheimer's is not a normal part of aging."

Q: Are there drugs that will ease symptoms?

A: "Only in a minimal way and with side effects that may be more unpleasant than Alzheimer's itself. Only a skilled doctor should prescribe the drugs, some of which cause aggressive behavior. Then they administer drugs to subdue the aggression. It soon becomes a delicate balance of one drug ameliorating another."

Q: Will there ever be a cure for Alzheimer's?

A: "In time, yes, but not soon. An aging population will

suffer symptoms, giving the impression that Alzheimer's is increasing. It isn't. The older patients are more likely to live long enough to suffer the symptoms."

Q: What is the significance of crop circles?
A: "They are the playful result of people with too much time on their hands."

Q: What happens to elected officials when they get to Washington, D.C.? They seem to get greedy and become dishonest.
A: "It is the nature of the system that newly elected officials are politically impotent unless they ally strongly with their parties. Thereby, the chase for money begins, to help them in the reelection process. Fortunately, on the truly crucial topics, most politicians vote for what is best for their constituents."

Q: Which book is more important: Koran, Bible, Torah?
A: "Each is important equally to the others. The underlying message is the same as already reported herein: love, not hate; care for others; be good in the eyes of the Creator."

Q: If we could live in love, would we ever feel fear?
A: "Fear comes with love. When a precious entity goes

forth to school, or war, or neighborhood shopping, those left behind suffer fear that something might happen to their loved one. One cannot love without fear of loss. It is the price we pay for loving someone."

Q: Should we worry about man's addiction to the use of technology such as smart phones, Blackberries, computers, electronic books and so forth?

A: "Not at all. Technology adapts the flow of time to a speed Man can see. Who would want to abandon television, radio, or telephone? The advance of technology will see Man to far-flung planets someday. Do not fear the advance of technology! It is Man's way of extending his brain. As Man masters technology it will lead him to master laws of the universe."

Q: If I have a difficult mother, will I be a difficult parent?

A: "As has been reported herein, a gentle, caring mother rears a gentle, caring child. The good and bad things about a parent tend to rub off on the child. Abuse is contagious. Raise your child with care; what you are, he or she will become."

Q: Can you name the Universal Laws?

A: "There are three, physical, mental, and spiritual: gravity, which gives the galaxies momentum, expansion, and contraction; repetition, in which all things recycle, including the souls of spirits; and the most important universal law, God, who should be praised and admired for that which has been created. Creative thought and expression are the result of the Divine Urge and are extensions of the Creator. Use these talents judiciously. To understand the laws of the universe is to understand God."

Q: Thank you, sir. Do you have anything else you want to say?

A: "Yes; don't show off.

The mind is both temporal and eternal, hence it is the builder. The soul is eternal because it is of God. By the manner in which you treat yourself, and your fellow man, so do you treat the Creator. Those things material are subject to decay. Those things that are temporal are material. Those things spiritual are everlasting."

Q: Where will the next great threat to America come from?

A: "From within."

Q: Will the threat be from Muslims?

A: "In many cases, yes."

Q: So the threat is ideological?

A: "Any threat is ideological."

Q: Will the threat bring down the United States Government?

A: "No. But the turmoil that will arise from the threat will further alter the lives of citizens. In the name of combating the ideological threat, citizens will be subjected to constant erosion of the values the founding fathers promulgated. Freedoms of various types will be diminished in the name of combating the theological threat. The citizens will forfeit privacy, the sanctity of the home against intrusion and search. As has happened in many nations where citizens suffered under chaotic conditions, the population voluntarily gives up individual freedoms for a dictator's promise of order in the society."

Q: Are you saying America will become a dictatorship?

A: "If citizens seek civil order over individual autonomy, it may happen."

Q: How do we avoid that?

A: "Be vigilant against political encroachment in the guise of making life safer.

We are through for the moment."

Q: Is it true that British schools are having drills to teach children how to handle UFO crashes?

A: "A few schools did this to spark the imagination of students."

Q: The lady who asked about crop circles says she cannot believe the phenomenon is perpetrated by any human. She believes extraterrestrials did it. She wants you to reconsider the question: who makes crop circles?

A: "The answer is the same. A harmless hoax designed to get attention."

Q: What should we title this tract?

A: "As may please you. The Return of Edgar Cayce is all right."

Q: What do you hope to accomplish with this exercise?

A: "To assure mankind that Man will survive. Nothing in the future is inviolate. The strength of human will power can alter events yet to come. Have faith in self and the Creator.

In a stable society the pendulum of human affairs swings in narrow arcs, always staying close to center point. In radical societies the pendulum swings from unyielding conservative to overly permissive liberalism.

If you would know tomorrow, study the past. Human events and attitudes are cyclic. In the extreme these include wars, social upheavals, and mass migrations. Shifts in attitudes include clothing fashions, moral turpitude, pomp and circumstance. Sin will be redefined. In every case there will be entities predicting an end to the world, citing current circumstances as proof.

Prosperity will come and go. Within the twenty-first century a worldwide depression will make nations shudder and subside. Localized wars will flare as populations vie for resources. Those best prepared to ride out the twenty-four years of deprivation will be entities who grow their own food. There will be a return to government-sponsored classes on canning foodstuffs, salvaging and recycling. Signs will appear in public places: Waste Not, Want Not.

Trade and barter will replace government-issued currency.

Affluence will be a cause for shame. The wealthiest segment of society will fear the lowest, retreating to armed compounds for security.

Obesity in the general population will diminish. The richest man will dress like a pauper to hide any sign of wealth or privilege."

Q: Is America destined for economic depression?
A: "It is inevitable and will circle the globe, brought on by irresponsible banks, greedy financial officers, and self-serving politicians."

Q: Is there anything an individual can do to fend off the crash?
A: "Pay off debts, learn to garden, be self-sufficient."

Q: What may Americans expect in the next fifty years?
A: "The Age of Overindulgence will pass. Honor, integrity, hard work, and generosity will be most prized among entities. Personal possessions will become less important. Private transportation will be more utilitarian and less ostentatious."

Q: In seventy-five years?
A: "There will be a return to family values. Youth will shelter and care for the old. Populations will rely less on government intervention. Long-distance travel will be mostly by public transportation. For the most part, walking, bicycling, and motor scooters will replace automobiles. Many municipalities will ban motorized vehicles from city centers. Shopping malls will fail as most personal purchases take place over the Internet."

Q: In the next hundred years?
A: "Nations without money cannot afford military adventures. Politicians advocating wars will be quickly removed from office. Only hunting rifles will be legal as assault weapons are outlawed. Violent crime will abate."

Q: One hundred twenty-five years?
A: "A period of little change as the world pauses to catch its breath. The birth rate will climb slightly to 1.2 children per family. The death rate will decline close to zero growth in most civilized nations."

Q: One hundred fifty years from now?
A: "The reappearance of individual innovation and personal ambitions will usher in a century of prosper-

ity. Financial markets will flourish. Societies will rebuild infrastructure. Printed books will be rare as most readers will use electronic publications displayed on handheld devices. Schoolchildren will wear Global Positioning System necklaces and bracelets. Minorities will become the majorities in North America. Bilingual candidates will most likely be elected. Handwriting will be lost to technological courses; students will learn to write and calculate on computers in place of pencil and paper. Handwritten love letters will become antiquities. Fully formed words will be reduced to abbreviations, acronyms and neologisms."

Q: Will Nazism arise again?
A: "Never like it was at the time of Hitler. Radical philosophies do not do well in reprise. Throughout history deposed despots have generally taken their dynasties to the graves with them. There are exceptions, of course; Genghis Khan's rule transferred to his sons, notably Kublai Khan, thereby extending his rule through hereditary linkage. The British monarchy has survived scandals, wars, and internecine purges. Elective papal monarchies have continued with the ties to Christianity. But usually, the end of a tyrant is the end of the dynasty. After Adolf Hitler, Nazis have been discredited and abandoned.

King Louis XIV, the tsars of Russia, and various attempts at absolute monarchies ended, and with their downfall went autocratic affiliations.

Nazism suffered at the hands of Hitler. In isolated places it will rise, only to sputter and extinguish. Anything that is absolute will eventually perish, as witness tyrants throughout history.

It is the nature of Man to seek the easiest route to peace; hence, he is often a follower and not a leader. And yet, as has been herein stated, under duress and social chaos, sometimes a despot seems the easiest route to tranquility."

Q: Will there be new dictatorships anywhere in the world?
A: "Indeed. Look for the seed of despotism in bodies of peoples torn by strife and hopelessly immersed in poverty; there will always be entities willing to forfeit individual freedoms in exchange for order in the living plane."

Q: Will any of those tyrants be the Antichrist?
A: "Satan thrives on discontent. Some politicians have learned the lesson well, showing up in troubled areas, exacerbating problems to further their personal standing."

Q: Are you speaking of specific people?

A: "Actions brand demigods. They will not last. There are few that power does not destroy.

We are through for the time being."

"Many of the inventions of modern-day Man are not new, but resurrections from thousands of Earth years ago. Atlanteans had electricity, radio, and television. They were capable of amplifying light rays for telescopes. Home heating and lighting were advanced beyond what Earth nations know today; wireless transmission of power for example. Out of that research evolved weapons of intense light, called death rays by entities of the present plane and light amplification known today as lasers. By recombination of molecular ores, Atlanteans developed metals unknown to Man today. Air- and watercraft were constructed of those metals, at first propelled by gas and electricity, but later by photocells from sunlight, captured and reflected by crystals.

From the subconscious minds of descendants of Atlantis, memories of past inventions will continue to appear in the activities of Man. Travel to distant galaxies will evolve from the early use of molecular propulsion; photocells will push spaceships farther and faster than ever imagined possible.

In the sacred temples of Poseidia on the great island of Parfa, holy founts of pure energy burned constantly. The fuel was the same photocells described here.

The destruction of Atlantis threw Man back to primitive roots where he struggled to survive. Thousands of Earth years passed. For lack of financial resources and human coordination, great ideas were forgotten. Only recently have societies gathered the wherewithal to master those ancient ambitions again.

In the world today there remains evidence of Atlantean influence, much of it not as yet recognized. Refugees fleeing destruction of their continent took Atlantean skills to newly settled lands in the form of architecture and worship of the sun, from which Atlantean power had once flowed.

The periods of exodus from Atlantis were separated by centuries. The five regions of Atlantis did not disappear all at once, but over time. The civilizations which fled to Spain and America after the first destruction were not the same as civilizations arriving in North Africa and

Central America after the next destruction. Even more removed from the others were Atlanteans who arrived in present-day Egypt and Yucatan.

These revelations were reported in readings by this entity as he existed in the Gregorian calendar year of 1933. They are repeated here to give Man perspective on his world of today. Knowing his past may help explain developments of the future.

It has been written in Ecclesiastes 1:9 what has been will be again, what has been done will be done again; there is nothing new under the sun.

It is a lesson Man has been loath to learn."

Q: Will there be changes in the Earth's surface?
A: "Change is the nature of the planet. It flows and grows and subducts, reshaped by shifting tectonic plates, washed by tidal waves and ground to sandy shores by ocean motion. Yes, there will be change."

Q: Will Earth shift on its axis?
A: "It has before and will again."

Q: Should we worry about it?
A: "Insofar as worry will do nothing to change geophysical events, be sensible. Don't live in the shade of an active

volcano; build your dwelling above the high water mark; be prepared for seasonal floods and meteorological disturbances. Otherwise, devote your energy to helping fellow beings."

Q: Is there any one thing we should say when we pray?
A: "Give thanks for blessings you enjoy. Pray for strength to be worthy of those who love you. Praise God for creations He has accomplished.

We are finished for the moment."

"The future is a lie posing as truth. Coming events are as variable as currents in a mountain brook. When making plans do not be motivated by fear. Think in terms of millennia, not decades. How will your actions be judged a century from now? Looking back on your earthly plane, how will you view your own life? Be brave. Do what is right."

Q: In your lifetime on Earth you gave readings in a self-induced hypnotic trance. When you awoke, you did not know what you had said. Do you now know all that you said?
A: "Yes."

Q: From the vantage of the Universal Wave, would you now say that in your lifetime you were a major prophet?
A: "Prophesy was not the goal of this entity. The motivation

was to help others, and through that endeavor, prophesies were revealed. As indicated, prophets (especially in the Biblical sense) brought messages from God and foretold the logical results of current trends. That was not the primary purpose of this entity's activities."

Q: Could you clarify a timeline from this reading for a thousand years?

A: "It is impossible; a thousand years with ten thousand possibilities! Man's will today can change something a thousand years from today; a thousand years from today Man's will can change it again. The only sure rules are Universal Laws as outlined herein."

Q: You have said, "The Lord will come when those who are His have made the way clear" for his return. Who are "those who are His?"

A: "The faithful, believers, those who worship God."

Q: You once said that China will be the cradle of Christianity. What about the resulting conflict with Buddha?

A: "There will be no conflict with Buddha. Buddha taught his disciples to be tolerant of other religions. When one lights a candle from the flame of another candle, the flame of the first candle does not lose its light. Instead, the two lights grow more brightly together. It is the same with the great religions of the world. Comparison of religions reveals many similarities. The four largest faiths—Christianity, Islam, Hinduism and Buddhism—offer much the same advice."

Q: When you refer to the Mosaic Law, what is that exactly?
A: "The laws given to the Israelites through Moses, beginning with the Ten Commandments. This includes rules of religious observance in the first five books of the Old Testament, the ancient Hebrew laws called the Torah."

Q: What did Jesus Christ learn from the prophetess Judy?
A: "The Essenes flourished in the three hundred years from 200 BC to 100 AD. It was a movement started by Jesus during his incarnation at that time. The question should be, what did Judy and Jesus learn from each other? It cannot be answered easily. Each entity taught the other in their various times on the earthly plane. The question is like asking what did you learn from your mother? The answer is everything."

Q: What should be the purpose of this book?
A: "Already it has been noted, the purpose is to reassure Man that the future is his to determine. Man will survive."

Q: Is there value to adding a teaspoon of baking soda to a glass of water daily?

A: "Only if you swallow it."

Q: Should I?

A: "The value of diets is singular: they make an entity conscious of what is taken into the body. Some fad diets are effective for weight loss, others for increased energy, another to calm nervous tensions. As has been stated many times, eat in moderation. Assimilate nutrients to strengthen muscle, bone, cardiovascular and nervous systems. Consume vegetables and fruits daily. It is best for one diurnal meal to be raw vegetables only. Favor alkaline over acidic. Restrict intake of meats to those low in fat and easily digested. With any diet, do not neglect exercise.

We are finished for the moment."

Q: How much of our personal/mortal consciousness do we retain after death?

A: "While on the earthly plane, every action, association, movement and thought is stored in the human brain. Not even the most trivial experience is lost. The capacity of the brain is infinite. All thoughts and experiences are carried into the Universal Wave upon demise of the body. At the point of transfer to a gaseous state, the entity undergoes a quick review of his most recent existence. He has time to consider his experience in human form. It is a period Catholics call purgatory. Eventually the mind sheds pride, prejudice, and ambition. The essence of the earthly plane is distilled to regrets. The time it takes to overcome regret varies with the individual, but eventually he forgives himself.

When spirit elects to return to human form, memories

of past lives are erased to allow for a new beginning. Man must learn all lessons again. The new life gives Man the opportunity to overcome failings from past lives, but he is very rarely aware of the burden he bears. Indian religions call the burdens karma, the effect of an action, good or bad, from a prior plane."

Q: Having forgiven ourselves during the purgatory aspects of existence, are we allowed to go on to heaven?
A: "Via many steps or stages, ultimately shame is discarded and through good deeds nirvana achieved, and the entity is freed of suffering (for past discretions). That is what may be termed as heaven, to be unburdened of anguish from karma."

Q: What if the entity has no regrets?
A: "What manner of being is this? All have regrets. Whatever his attitude on the Earth plane, upon arrival on the Universal Wave every spirit sees the errors of past judgment."

Q: Even tyrants like Hitler, Stalin, and others who caused such human suffering?
A: "Especially those spirits."

Q: Where is Hitler now?

A: "In the presence of millions of spirits, begging forgiveness."

Q: Did John really write Revelation?

A: "Which John? He identified himself several times. He said he was on the Island of Patmos when he had his first vision, thus he is often referred to as John of Patmos, and others say it was John the Apostle. Then there were the predictions of John the Baptist. Which John? This is like the debate: Did Francis Bacon write Shakespeare's plays? (No.)

Most major literary works are the result of many emendations and therefore the imprint of editors must come into consideration. Not only language but the message itself was altered slightly by various entities that translated, transcribed, and edited these works. Who knows the thoughts in an author's head? John of Patmos may have drawn on predictions of John the Baptist. The Apostle John had a hand (and a different view) in the final book now called Revelation.

If as John said, Revelation came in visions, was not the author also one or more of his friends?

Man requires parables to explain that which he does

not understand. How was Man created? Adam was incarnated from Amilius, the preceding spirit thought-form; division took place making woman to share existence with man. How does the Master explain the process to entities who are as children, uneducated in molecular science?

Why is it any less miraculous that a single cell is created from the swamp of nutrients required to make life, after which the cell divides into two, and then four, finally becoming a mass that is the first creature? One species evolved into two and then there were four. Ultimately from that one-cell beginning, all of God's earthly creatures came into being. In Earth time it took millions of years, but that is but a twinkle in universal time. The miracle of life is no less mysterious and magnificent on the cellular level. It is matter touched by the Supreme Being. Explain that process to a child! It is simpler to say there was Adam, and from Adam came Eve and from the two of them came children and thus humanity was born.

What made the universe? There was one cell and it became two; it is the same process on a larger scale. Science validates God. The more learned Man, the more will he become convinced of God's existence.

The material body that is Man has the same basic structure as all other animals. Animals are kin to plants.

As has been stated herein, a single molecule is the universe in miniature. There are more molecules in your body than there are stars in the heavens. The molecule is constructed of atoms, as few as two and as many as hundreds of millions.

Everything is constructed of atoms. The human body is not so different from all other things, liquid or solid, living or inert. Except for variations in shape and function, all things are built of the same blocks. The universe is a miracle. Truly God is great. Praise Him for what He has done!

We are through for the moment."

"By the year 2042 bee populations will have declined to catastrophic levels, killed off worldwide by a deadly combination of causes. Scientists blame a fungus, a virus, inbreeding, and pesticides for the decline of domestic and wild bees. Without bees to pollinate crops, farm production declines. To compensate for the loss of produce, growers increase use of chemical fertilizers.

It is true that the decline of bees is the result of multiple causes, but the primary reason is indiscriminate spraying to eradicate pests such as mosquitoes. In tropical and subtropical areas where mosquitoes are a problem for humans, annual spraying has become commonplace. Killing the mosquitoes also kills other insects. As a result, the food chain is disrupted. Birds that normally feed on insects have less to eat and the avian numbers decline accordingly.

The culprits are golf courses fighting broad-leaved invaders on the greens, homeowners killing weeds and farmers spraying fields to eliminate pests. Bumblebees, honeybees, and wild bees are unintentional victims of these widespread uses of pesticides.

When the root causes are finally identified, in 2042, further attempts to eliminate pests will also have deleterious effects on insects such as butterflies, reducing their numbers to the point of extinction. Birds will suffer, as will amphibians, and as a result by 2050 mankind will be struggling to reintroduce native creatures to local environments.

Man has disrupted the natural order of life. So-called walking catfish, nutria, kudzu, killer bees, the spread of gypsy moths, Asian carp in the Great Lakes, exotic reptiles released by pet owners in the Everglades, fire ants brought to Alabama by merchant ships, water hyacinths choking Florida canals, and commercial destruction of habitats are unsettling the scheme of nature. Frogs are declining around the world, reducing some populations to the brink of utter annihilation. Clear-cutting the rain forests has drastically reduced the number of jungle creatures.

Mankind will reap the sad results of wanton attempts to control insects considered as pests. Tourists in bathing suits may be more comfortable without mosquitoes and biting flies, but the ecological price is the destruction of all insects in the region, reduction of birds, and failure of flowers and crops except when pollinated by human hands.

By the time this entity returns to the Earth plane in 2050, these environmental calamities will be uppermost in the minds of agricultural laboratory scientists. These problems will be further aggravated by the decline of potable waters as aquifers are poisoned by chemical run-off. Rocky Mountain streams, once pure and safe drinking water, are now polluted by melting snows which have absorbed toxic chemicals from the air.

An international effort to cleanse air and waters of the world will be in full swing by 2070, but the attempts will be frustrating and often futile.

The importation of biological enemies to combat destructive pests will often introduce new pests to the environment.

The year 2100 will be a turning point, when Man admits defeat by the natural forces that have evolved over hundreds of years. In most cases the best defense against nature is to leave it alone.

Two factors will become major debates for North Americans by the year 2090. The increasing tide of Spanish-speaking peoples will change the balance of races, alter political demographics, and shift the emphasis of minority education. At the same time, all things of Spanish flavor will become the major influence in music, theater, and American cuisine. America will be stronger for it.

In the year 2095, recent immigrants in America will join those who tried to keep them out, and together they will fight to halt further illegal immigration. This has happened before in the case of European immigrants who gained political power and tried to staunch further encroachment by new arrivals from Ireland, Germany, the Baltic States, Poland, and Greece.

2105: Drug-resistant pathogens will provoke a major scandal in the pharmaceutical industry brought about by accusations that those organizations knew they were immunizing diseases against their own products. At which point the pharmaceutical giants will lobby the U.S. Government for huge sums of money to develop new drugs to meet the threat. Antibacterial soaps will be banished.

2110: A new species of termite will be a major problem in the building industry. These termites will gnaw through concrete and will not be affected by the usual poisons. Entire cities will be ravaged by an insect that reduces any wooden structure to shreds.

In the five hundred years since 1500, three hundred species of birds have become extinct. By the year 2140, another 1100 species will be critically endangered. Destruction of habitats will hasten the process as species vanish forever.

At the time of Atlantis, 10,000 years ago, the American mastodon, the American lion, American camel, American equine, dire wolf, cave lion, giant beaver, and ground sloth existed in what is now known as North America. They have all become extinct. The steady extinction of various species of animals and plants continues with shrinking habitats, global warming, and the predatory practices of Man. The American bison was almost lost but has since recovered due to conservation efforts. Do not wantonly kill anything.

2150: DNA reconstruction of extinct animals will succeed. The Tasmanian tiger will be resurrected with DNA drawn from museum specimens and injected into the embryo of a mouse. When the cells become active the Tasmanian tiger embryo will be transferred to a species of domestic cat from whence it will be removed by Caesarian section.

2175: Similar experiments will be tried in secret with human DNA but the attempts will fail and public condemnation will deprive the laboratories of government funds. Still, in private, attempts will continue in isolated locations around the world. In two hundred years the efforts will succeed and a reconstituted DNA child will be born. The fetus will live seventeen days before dying for want of better lungs. It will be another two centuries before the experiment works, at which point Man will consider himself equal to God. It is a dangerous premise inviting intervention by the Creator.

Eventually, when intergalactic travel is perfected, the DNA of human and other animals will be sent to other worlds where the result can be brought to maturation and studied. In time, humans of various worlds will be discovered to have originated from a common ancestor, and this will be taken as proof there is a Supreme Being who spread mankind throughout thousands of galaxies. Fundamentalist Earth religions will collapse as men on the earthly plane realize egocentric ideas have been misguided.

The universal law of cause and effect should be a cause for quiet reflection. A volcano erupts on one side of the world and it has a direct and immediate effect on the opposite side of the globe. As is herein written, good deeds come back to you. Generosity returns generosity. Likewise, misdeeds beg retaliation in kind.

Therefore think before you act. Is this something you want to come back to you? Make moves gently, soften the tone of your voice and speak with tenderness. Weigh the intent of words you speak and cast them carefully as you would hurl darts. Once thoughts are unleashed they have a life of their own, and remember that which you think, you are. The place to shape verbal slings and arrows is within, before you speak.

Live life by two commandments: love God, and love thy neighbor. Truly these are the greatest of the Biblical rules. This does not mean you should spend your existence face down in constant supplication. Live life! Get up and be about your existence. But live the commandment with each breath and every action. Do not plot to avenge a wrong, but forgive the transgressor. Don't burden yourself with a grudge against a fellow entity. Be kind to those less fortunate than yourself. Do these things and the Creator will be well pleased.

Being generous is more than giving to charities. It is giving of self as well. A forgiving attitude and generosity of spirit have the weight of gold. A benevolent outlook will shine through to your fellow man, and nobody will benefit more than will you yourself.

The most damaging threat to mankind is the collective

attitude that the world is beyond repair. Immersed in bad news, surrounded by disasters, discouraged by financial reversals, suffering deflections from ambitious goals, it is easy to become depressed and discouraged. Back up, take a deep breath and look at the reality of the current plane.

Yes, there is hunger. Yes, there are wars and pestilence. Suffering comes in many forms. But hardships and deprivations of today are no worse than those of years past.

Americans have more miles of good highways than any nation in the world. Medical services are excellent. Wars are being fought in other lands, not on U.S soil. No longer are women in the U.S. denied the right to vote or to own property. More citizens enjoy equality of status than ever before. Violent crime has diminished. It is not government policy to seize citizens and cause them to disappear forever. Public executions are a thing of the past. Religions flourish without dictating public policy to the body politic. Through the American courts, citizens have the means to redress abuse. The majority of homes are safe from invasion. Most cities have police protection, fire departments, libraries, and hospitals.

There are conditions about which to complain and always will be. It is not a perfect world, but in many ways America is the best country on the planet. Social ills are soon confronted. Somebody somewhere is constantly striving to improve this or that flaw in the fabric of American life.

America is the cornucopia pouring forth abundance to other nations. Americans are the best hope for world peace. Her people are generous.

Man will survive the millennium in great measure because of America."

Q: What is the difference between spirit and soul?
A: "The soul of Man is a manifestation of God. God made the souls to be his companions, endowed them with divine attributes and gave to them free will. The souls, still in spirit form, chose self-aggrandizement to the extent they became entangled in matter. Their downfall was a disappointment to the Creator. God Himself oversaw the making of Adam who was the first begotten of the Father. He was encased in matter but he was the perfect man. Adam likewise fell.

Spirit is the primary beginning, the first cause, the motivating influence. God is spirit. The mind of Man is an effect of spirit. Spirit is an essence without form, as gas, odor, and wind; time and space are concepts created by spirits.

Before birth there are four levels of spirit, which is to say four levels of awareness. The fourth level gives Man insights close to godlike, including the continuum of time and space without limits. But upon birth, the fourth spirit is lost and Man then has the three spirits of human form, including knowledge of who he is and what he is; the three levels of spirit give Man insight into his mortality, his connection to the Creator, and some understanding of the three-dimensional world of the Earth plane. The spirit of Man is the creative aspect of his existence. When Man dies, he regains that fourth level of spirit as herein described.

Soul is the residue of spirit, the reservoir of Man's experience, the personality he has been. Soul is the heart of the person. People say he is a good soul. Bless his soul, they say.

The soul is that which the Supreme Being gives to every entity or individual in the beginning. It is the soul that is seeking the home again or place of the Creator. The subconscious mind is an attribute of the soul. When Man first entered the earthly plane, his soul was a spiritual entity in which there was embedded a spark of Divine Fire. It was Man not God who brought into existence the physical bodies in which the soul now lodges while on Earth.

In other words, soul is the luggage in which Man transports the sum total of his earthly existences.

We are finished for the time being."

Q: Is it necessary to enter the Earth plane as matter in order to advance the soul?

A: "Not necessary, but existence in the Earth plane, or the plane of some similar world, will help in the development of soul. To advance the psychic soul one must undergo the growth of experience, whether on the planet Earth, or any of the similar worlds available to the entity. Growth is attained through resisting selfish lusts, ego-enhancing pursuits, and temptations to enrich self through dishonest acts. Knowing that fire burns we do not thrust a hand into flames. Knowing the karmic result of sin makes it easy to resist evil. In human form, we know better and yet often yield to temptations. Denying self the pleasures of transgressions is the way to psychic growth."

Q: From the Universal Wave, considering a return to

the Earth plane, do we have a choice of where we will be born and under what circumstances?

A: "From the vantage of the spirit plane, we know what experiences we need to progress. We select a general existence that will best fulfill our karmic needs, male, female, one race or another. Having been born to the existence and deprived of the overview of the fourth level of spiritual awareness, we are less philosophical about the ordeal we suffer. Unaware of how we got there, suffering accordingly, this is the grit of spiritual advancement. Make the most of your existence; serve the needs of others, follow the commandments, and in the twinkling of the cosmic eye you will be back to the Universal Wave in a more advanced spiritual state."

(From a woman who lives in New Zealand):

Q: If it is true that I as a woman create my own universe, and my husband creates his own universe, and these are in conflict with one another, how is the reality of the conflict resolved? (We are now divorced.)

A: "There is no conflict; these are parallel universes—you may share them or not but that does not alter your universe or his. In your sleep if you dream, and in his sleep he dreams, and neither of you dream of the other, in no way do these dreams clash with one another. Upon awakening, you are together (or not) and the reality of the Earth plane is established once again. It is possible for a family of several entities to each have a universe of their own, interlocking or separate from one another. The choice of universe is up to you, in the spirit realm and in the Earth world as well."

Q: Are Americans in good hands with the present politicians?

A: "As has been indicated herein, those who are dedicated will continue to act on behalf of their constituents. Almost all politicians are good representatives when first elected to office. Over a period of time they become frustrated by an inability to accomplish what they set out to achieve. Cynicism sets in and the politician begins to think more and more about what must be done to get reelected to office. The people who elect the officials are also responsible for the onset of bitterness that politicians begin to suffer. With angry correspondence, insulting face-to-face confrontations, letters to newspaper editors assailing the politicians, constituents induce a state of resentment. Eventually the disillusioned politician feels he has given more than voters deserve. The art of politics is compromise. All too often people feel betrayed by the politician's compromises, when in fact that is the only way anything will be accomplished. The candidate may even learn to despise the people who put him in office. This is not new. Citizens insulted the first meetings of the Roman Senate, about 500 BC, when elected representatives were chosen from the richest members of the Roman Republic."

Q: Another question about reincarnation. If we have a choice about where and with whom we wish to be born, how do we end up with so many of the relations we've had in prior incarnations?

A: "Although it may not be the wisest choice, entities tend to go where they know other entities. Thus relatives from the past tend to come together in the same proximity. Entities may renew connections with past relations, but not necessarily be linked in the same way. Fathers become brothers, brothers become mothers, and sisters are males in a mixed bag of blood relatives. Connecting again with a former relative may be a good karmic lesson if the previous relationship was abandoned without resolving troublesome issues."

Q: Are you saying we can't deliberately team up in the same way with past loved ones even if we want to?

A: "Not at all. You may elect to meet old loves and cruise

through an existence with no karmic challenge. But the mortar of psychic building is trial, not contentment. Adversity is the way to build character and improve karmic standing."

Q: You're saying we have to suffer to advance. Is this why God-fearing people of the Bible suffered such horrible lives?
A: "Heat of a furnace anneals steel and human suffering tempers the soul."

Q: Why would anyone follow Christ since to do so guaranteed a miserable ending? Why didn't Jesus protect his disciples?
A: "We remember those who suffered. The agony of crucifixion is an indelible image imprinted upon the consciousness of mankind. There were countless souls who encountered no pain at all. Their stories are seldom recalled. Keeping the faith throughout torment is a test to be admired. This is not to say you cannot have happiness; indeed you can. But remember the poet's line that luck's a chance and trouble's sure. Bad things are bound to happen in life. When they do, meet them with confidence. Know that your soul is maturing with the experience. Do not abandon hope. Persevere. Have faith. That is how the

soul is strengthened and karmic debt is resolved.

God does not want you to suffer. He wants you to be happy. But joy is best savored after the sting of tragedy. Be strong. Endure. Good times will come again."

Q: You make life sound like a wretched experience.
A: "For some it is. God bless them.

About the human condition there is much to be admired. The body is an intricate assimilation of blood, bone, and muscle; the brain has the capacity to read a book, watch a movie, and carry on a conversation all at the same time. Truly Man is a reflection of his Maker. Look what he has accomplished! As of today there are 1,003, 322 words in the English language making it possible to say precisely what a writer wishes to express. Among all animals of the world, Man has the remarkable ability to create his own reality. He is a tender lover and an awesome warrior, an inventor, builder, dreamer, and realist.

Man is destined for even greater accomplishments. He yearns and learns and advances with experience. He is a tutor and mentor, lifting himself and his society with every incarnation.

He has a sense of humor.

What more magnificent creature could any organism

be than Man? Look at his cities of towering buildings, subterranean arteries, grids of power, and cross-country transports. He is an astounding success in so many pursuits, bending the world to his means, and now he reaches for the stars.

Every entity should be proud to be a part of the human species. He is aptly named *Homo sapiens*, from the Latin meaning wise or knowing man. He is a creature who is self-aware, rational and introspective. Through science, mythology, religion, and philosophy, mankind struggles to understand and control the environment. The talents of Man do not perish with the passing of his lifetime. To the next generation he bequeaths lessons through art and literature, thereby advancing society steadily.

Whatever his weaknesses on an individual level, Man is well suited to find his way home. He has extended his earthly lifespan and will continue to do so. Someday his heirs will live twice as long as entities today. They will conquer disease, overcome antisocial behavior, and master latent capabilities of the brain.

In the animal kingdom Man alone dresses himself, cooks with fire, and adjusts his environment for comfort with heat and cooling fans. He is a curious creature, constantly asking the names of things and wanting to know why and how. He is 98.4 percent identical to the chimpanzees, and yet Man has developed a brain twice as large as that of his primate cousin.

Man can talk.

Imagine the tribal reaction when a human burst into song for the first time 50,000 years before the present day. Surely a voice so pure and melodic must have held an audience in rapture.

Humans have explored ocean depths, Antarctica, and the highest mountains. They have walked upon the moon, and other heavenly bodies have been visited by manmade objects. In two hundred years, from 1800 to now, the population of Man has increased from one billion to over six billion. The human animal is the most numerous mammal on Earth.

Rejoice that you are man! Glory to God and blessed be we who are crafted in His image."

Q: Is there another me living in a parallel universe?
A: "The idea of a parallel universe is the fancy of fiction writers who have seized upon probabilities and made them exact. As reported in a reading in June, 1941, even if there were a parallel universe; no two leaves of a tree are the same, no two blades of grass are the same, and no two

systems have the same awareness; neither are they parallel. Can you conceive of the influences that would have to be the same to create a duplicate of self? Precisely the same friends, family, environs, all at exactly the same time; it would be a mathematical impossibility. You are unique in the universe, one of a kind and constantly evolving. His hand is upon you and builds no other similar."

Q: Is a large earthquake due in California soon?
A: "There will be warnings prior to a devastating shake. Eruptions will occur around the Pacific in Japan, New Zealand, Chile, and Alaska, with ascending violence. Then California will be jolted, followed by Wyoming and Missouri. Scientists are on the verge of mastering earthquake predictions with a system that has not yet been fully appreciated. Several pending quakes will be recognized by a private enterprise before seismologists accept the premise of predicting upheavals by 'singing' rocks. That is to say, under increasing pressure, subterranean rock mass emits an increasingly shrill tone that can be detected prior to a shift of tectonic plates. Meantime, do not reside in rickety buildings. Do not build on shifting soil such as reclaimed dump sites that may liquefy under pressure.

Do not live for disaster. Be prudent, but live each day to the fullest. As already reported, do not encumber your life with fears of future disruptions.

The major faults in California are not tectonic plates, but human. Much-admired men will succumb to sexual intrigue and fall from grace in the eyes of the public. These are the very enticements that have destroyed the careers of great entities of the past.

In the activities of mankind there are too many variables to make accurate predictions. The flow of human opinions can swing widely on any subject thereby changing the dynamics of action and reaction. Compared with guessing the future of Man, predicting geological events is easier. As for earthquakes in California, keep an eye on the Pacific horizon."

Q: Please define esoteric and exoteric religions.
A: "Esoteric means that which is for a limited or select group. It is information that might be understood by only a few people. Exoteric is unlimited, something that would be for a wide audience. Reincarnation as believed by the Essenes was an esoteric subject that the general population might not have understood. Therefore the matter was deleted from the Bible and subsequently eliminated

from Christian teaching. The story of Adam and Eve is an exoteric explanation of the origin of mankind, widely repeated in many religions."

Q: Explain what is happening in the Bermuda Triangle to cause so many ships and planes to disappear.
A: "The 500,000 square miles enveloped in the area from Puerto Rico to Miami to Bermuda, the so-called Bermuda Triangle, encompasses very deep and cold trenches of the Atlantic Ocean. The current flows fast, sweeping from south to north. If a ship sinks or a plane crashes, as it sinks to a depth of as much as ten thousand feet, the ocean currents strew evidence over a vast region. Therefore there is little or no physical evidence found. In the same waters lurk many sharks that devour human remains. The overall impression is that planes and water-craft and human beings have simply vanished.

The causes are varied. In the area being described, cold air and warm air collide. Fog can appear suddenly in a dense cloud that reduces visibility to zero. From the depths of the sea huge bubbles of gas may break loose and rise thousands of feet to the surface. It is flammable methane that may cause an airplane to explode. At the moment gas bubbles rise, the water loses buoyancy and a ship can sink instantly. Freak waves a hundred feet high have been generated by weather, geologic conditions, and thermal currents bursting onto the scene.

A similar set of events occur in the Devil's Triangle off the Pacific Coast of Japan, with similar results—planes and craft disappear without a trace."

Q: Then the cause of disappearances is not from anything left from Atlantis or aliens from other planets? What about reports of compasses which swing inaccurately in the region?

A: "After ten thousand years, most things left from Atlantis have been covered with barnacles and rotted by salt waters. The loss of compass readings is not confined to the areas discussed here. Magnetic north has to be calculated by oceangoing travelers and sometimes they get it wrong. Magnetic north changes naturally from time to time."

Q: There's nothing occult happening in the Bermuda Triangle?

A: "As viewed from here, there is nothing occult happening in the area. Occult or psychic influences fall in the same category as conspiracy theories, old seafaring myths, and superstitions. Man is easily spooked when out of his element; panicked sailors have been known to jump into the sea when terrorized by ghosts aboard."

Q: How many readings did you give in your earthly incarnation?
A: "A total of 14,246 readings were transcribed and retained at A.R.E. in Virginia Beach, Virginia. Many other readings preceded the readings that were recorded by stenographers; those have been lost."

Q: Is the Biblical account of the Tower of Babel accurate?
A: "The account of the Tower of Babel is accurate to a great degree. Constructed of sun-dried and kiln-baked mud bricks, with bitumen as mortar and to make the structure impervious to water, the Tower is called a ziggurat by present-day archeologists. At the time of building, seven or eight centuries after the Biblical flood, the world population was fewer than tens of thousands of entities, many of whom were descendants of Noah struggling to establish order out of a demolished past.

It has always been the nature of Man to blame the Creator for widespread destruction. As already indicated, God does not plot to make Man suffer. Natural disasters are not the handiwork of God. The flood was the aftermath of the sinking of Atlantis and a massive wave called today a tsunami, foretold to Noah by his angel friends who warned him to build an ark. That much is Biblical history recognized by most major religions.

Migrating together after the Biblical flood, citizens of the known world spoke the same language with a minimum of words, and they numbered less than tens of thousands. On the plain of Shinar in Babylon, construction of the tower began as a refuge in the event of another flood. The first building continued for forty-three years. Frightened and clustered together, future generations added to the building until it reached seven levels high, the tallest manmade structure in the world until completion of the Eiffel Tower 3,500 years later.

Many times the tower was struck by deadly and destructive lightning. The Mesopotamians took this as a sign from an angry God. Eventually they abandoned Babylon and migrated to other lands. Separated and isolated by distance, from the original one language known as Sumerian came Gothic, Celtic, and Persian: languages known now as Indo-European. Today there are three thousand languages and billions of people speaking them.

It should not surprise self that dispersal developed many languages. American dialects vary from New Orleans to New York to Chicago and Georgia. Exposure to national radio and television has reversed our linguistic isolation. We are moving once again toward one language, which will be accomplished in a few thousand years."

Q: Will the Bermuda triangle shift as ocean currents shift?

A: "The so-called Bermuda Triangle has never been set except by the imagination of Man."

Q: Will troubles between the Palestinians and Israel be resolved soon?

A: "This is a dispute that goes back so far many of the participants cannot remember why they are fighting. Fueled by widespread unemployment and ancient rivalries, settlement of differences will not occur until both sides accept concessions from the other. The contention is as much economic as societal. Peace between the contenders for at least one full generation, and possibly two or three, will be necessary to end the fighting. When today's child looks upon his ancestors with bemused detachment, peace will become final. Meantime, raids and retaliation continue.

The sad side of human relations is Man's love of warfare. Young men eagerly volunteer for military service at the first sign of trouble. During sporting events fans scream for the murder of their opponents. This does not happen in cooking classes and flower clubs. Man is drawn to warfare, particularly when the participants are impoverished and idle with nothing else to do but fight. To make matters worse, nonparticipants cheer them on. The combatants are idealized and death makes them martyrs thereby luring new young recruits into the forays.

Man loves contention and glamorizes fighting. When there is no war, Man plays combative sports like football or soccer.

The key to peace between Palestine and Israel is gainful employment and the prosperity that will result. Well-to-do and well-fed citizens do not jeopardize families and property with military hostilities.

Peace begins in the home. Loving families do more to promote world peace than any statesman or military alliance.

Remember: in Him is the light and the light is the light of the world.

By whatever faith you seek the Father, pray earnestly and you will be heard. Reserve time each day to meditate, and thank the Creator for all that He has given to you. Blessed be those who honor God. He is everywhere. You will be heard."

(Long pause...)

Q: Do you have anything you'd like to add, Mr. Cayce?

A: "The ills of mankind will be cured when entities love one another. Each to another and all of them together can change the course of coming events with mutual respect. Be not negative in your outlook, but gaze upon your fellow man with a positive attitude. Look for the best and not the worst in every encounter. Know that you are having a direct and indelible effect on each life you touch. Therefore treat them gently and be forgiving. Love thy neighbor and that love will come back to you in countless folds."

Q: You are answering everybody else's questions. May I ask a couple of personal questions?

A: "Personal aggrandizement is not the purpose here."

Q: Will this writing project be a success?

A: "Success in what regard? Spreading a message? Remuneration? As indicated repeatedly, temporal questions are not the purpose here. How strong is the anchor and what gale can you withstand? The greater success brings a greater storm. Be careful what you wish for."

"The twenty-first century will be a pivotal hundred years for America. The Age of Overindulgence is past and yet Americans refuse to give up their grand life-styles. No new taxes, the people demand; no cuts in social and medical services. A financial crisis looms and weak-willed politicians refuse to meet the problem realistically. The result is inevitable: mounting inflation as the government borrows from foreign powers and meets domestic shortfall by printing more currency.

There will be shortages in petroleum, particularly automotive fuels. Prices will continue to rise. Industry will falter. Plastics will give way to fabrics derived from cotton, ramie, and bamboo.

The higher cost of transport will add to the cost of food.

Two centuries of abusing the environment will begin to tell. Salt domes in the Gulf Coast area will show signs of leaking radioactive waste. Western caves used as nuclear dump sites will seep pollutants that have a half-life of thousands of years. Aquifers will be poisoned by agricultural chemical runoff. Fouled farmlands will be abandoned due to contamination. All of these calamities will be the result of attempts to maintain the lavish living of citizens who continue to insist on holding the status quo.

Water will become the most precious commodity, ascending in price and descending in availability. Rationing will be more commonplace. Desalination of seawater will become imperative. Conservation will become law with severe penalties for wasting liquid resources.

The necessary changes in public attitudes will begin in elementary school as children are taught to resent past extravagances of their elders. 'Waste not want not' will be a catch phrase displayed on billboards, in classrooms, and emblazoned on T-shirts and theater screens. Young people will be recognized for their reclamation and recycling efforts. Public opinion is like a mighty seagoing vessel; it does not turn quickly. But it will turn.

Meanwhile, Man will survive."

Q: What is life like on other planets inhabited by man?
A: "Life on other planets is much like it is on the Earth

plane. Some globes are larger and inhabitants weigh more, others are smaller and humans weigh less. The biosphere is similar to Earth. In some worlds oxygen is richer while elsewhere other gases are more prevalent. It is comparable to the polluted city air of Los Angeles where millions of entities continue to live and work. Other worlds have rarefied air identical to that of the Rocky Mountains. Multicellular organisms produce their own food from inorganic matter by photosynthesis, taking in carbon dioxide and returning oxygen as a waste product, which in turn is breathed by the animal kingdom.

Temperatures vary depending on the distance from the solar sources comprising the central axis around which planets orbit. Only if the mean distance of the planet and its sun is similar to the 93 million miles that separates our earth from its sun will the planet receive amounts of light and heat comparable to ours. The fragile envelope in which life can exist may range from the cold of Earth's polar extremity to the heat of equatorial regions. The diameter of the Earth's sun is approximately 865,000 miles and its mass is 330,000 times that of Earth. On some other worlds the sun may be larger or smaller with distances that compensate for the increase or decrease of solar effects. Man is a resilient creature capable of adapting to radical environments, as he has done on the Earth plane.

The social accomplishments and failures are similar to those of Earth. On the planes where human life has existed much longer than on Earth, with a few exceptions, many societal problems have been resolved. The density of population depends almost directly on the availability of resources. Human vices seem to know no intergalactic limits. Greed, ego, envy, and hatred generate crimes, hence a judicial system to deal with them.

In the same manner as Earth, there is affection, familial affinities, and the beauty of art and music. For the more fortunate there is abundance, serenity, good health, and happiness. In the case of more mature societies, uncivilized and dangerous entities are not allowed. The lifespan may be hundreds of years in Eden-like environs. Or, in radically less-advanced societies, the humanoids are primitive, given to wars and dissension.

Most entities elect to return to the same worlds from which they came. Individuals often relate to places where they have been born, lived, and died over many lifetimes. Good or bad, it is home.

The evolution of a world is much like that of its individuals. From infancy a toddler learns to walk, becomes cognizant of others, and grows into rambunctious adolescence. Dreams give way to reality. The psyche bends to the pressures of peers and family. Ultimately the core becomes adult. Experience brings wisdom and maturity. So it is with the world plane. Some planets are reckless juveniles; others are old and wise.

We are finished for the time being."

Q: Will a woman arise in the Middle East to become a proponent of education and the rights of women?

A: "The question strikes to the very heart of the cure for Middle Eastern turmoil. Woman was created to leaven the masculine propensity to impulsive actions. There have always been women leaders, at least as far back as 3000 BC, when Egyptian queens ruled. In 2500 BC, Ku-baba governed the Mesopotamian state of Ur. In more modern times, in 1960 when Sri Lanka was Ceylon, the first female prime minister was elected. Isabel Perón of Argentina became the first woman president in 1974. By 1999, Sweden had more female ministers than male; in the Finnish government, six of ten ministers were women. As of the twenty-first century, there were thirty-two female leaders in thirty countries. The United Kingdom, Denmark, and the Netherlands all had queens. Female presidents hold office in twelve nations ranging from Argentina to Switzerland. Women leaders are in the ascendancy worldwide.

Where women rule, generally speaking, peace reigns.

If the present trend continues, America will have a woman president, possibly of African descent, within the present century.

Worldwide, women have had a hard time achieving national leadership positions. Benazir Bhutto and Indira Gandhi are two of the more famous woman killed by political opponents, but there have been others, like Maria Elena Moyano of Lima, Peru.

To answer the question directly, there will be women elected to leadership roles in the Middle East, but it will be a full century before any woman in that area achieves power and avoids assassination long enough to alter the flow of her nation. Palestine, Syria, Egypt, Iraq, and Iran will have women leaders in the next two hundred years.

Will they inculcate a respect for the rights of women? Some will and some won't. Education of women will improve, lapse, and improve again as Muslim societies slowly adapt to the reality of the day.

When women do achieve parity with men in the desert countries, peace will at last be established and hold fast. How soon? There are too many variables within the human condition to predict an answer."

Q: Will there be a World War III in my lifetime?

A: "The war is current and ongoing. The conflict is driven by ideological and theological motives coupled with economic ambitions, similar to past wars with religious overtones such as the Islamic expansion, the Crusades, the Thirty Years War, the French Revolution, and the Iranian Revolution.

Current battles against terrorism have the potential to flare into global conflict. From the vantage of the Universal Wave such a war does not appear likely at this time, although battles will persist for decades under one pretext or another.

Man has been fighting Man since the beginning of Man. It is not likely to end until the Coming of the Savior and the final battle before the Resurrection, metaphorically speaking. Resurrection is a term fabricated by humans. Spirits do not die and thus they cannot be raised from the dead.

For the overall benefit of mankind, culling the herd would ease the strain on society. Winnowing wheat does more than remove chaff. It also eliminates weevils and other pests. In the broad scheme of things, thinning the masses would be good. Whether by war or disease, bringing overpopulation under control would have benefits. Fewer people mean less demand for scarce resources; also, world war tends to generate a sobering appreciation for life.

The one thing mankind can count on is the continued existence of Man. The prospect of shifting power centers should not trouble the citizens. Dominant empires have come and gone over the centuries. The rise and fall of great nations is going to happen. America has had her day in the sun and for the most part she handled it well. There are events for which the nation can be ashamed: usurpation of Native Americans from their tribal homes, slavery, racism, and occasional wars for purely selfish reasons. But no other assembly of citizens can be prouder of themselves for overcoming past injustices.

In the century just ended, Americans championed democratic reforms at home and abroad. For good and righteous reasons, the blood of patriotic youths soaked the soil on battlefields around the globe. Having defeated her enemies, America lifted them to their feet and financed recovery of Japan and Germany.

No nation ever did more for the health and welfare of others. Thanks to the United States, many diseases have been vanquished. Advances in agriculture managed to produce food for a burgeoning world populace. People live longer more productive lives in large part because of American generosity.

Americans are quick to forgive, always available to assist their friends. No other nation will so quickly bristle militarily if one or two of her citizens are wronged anywhere in the world.

The U.S. legal system is available to every citizen when inequities have been perpetrated against them. Any American can go to court for any reason if he thinks he has been wronged.

Even the U.S. Constitution is a living document, subject to amendments as circumstance may dictate.

In the face of disaster anywhere in the world, Americans donate money from their personal income. Additionally, Americans give of themselves through organizations like the Peace Corps.

It is only in recent years that American politicians have allowed U.S. generosity to slip. Of the twenty-two richest nations, the United States ranks last in the quality and quantity of foreign aid offered to poor nations. American politicians tell their citizens that the U.S. gives the most aid of any nation and it is true. But the government demands that recipients use American money to purchase U.S. products, thereby using U.S. aid to further U.S. commercial interests. It is a practice that breeds hatred for America.

Denmark, Norway, the Netherlands, and Sweden allocate more of their gross domestic product for foreign aid; relative to gross domestic product America is the stingiest of them all. Over the last several decades, America's generosity has been more and more militaristic. The U.S. has become selective in funding, giving mostly to middle-income Middle East nations, with Israel receiving the greatest sum.

But this will change.

The poor have always been more generous than the wealthy. As American influence and prosperity wane, by the end of the century, the U.S. will be more accommodating to the less fortunate.

Individual Americans are generous. They are also easily deceived by their politicians. Until the perfidy of the President Richard Nixon, by and large Americans accepted the word of their elected representatives. After Nixon, skepticism cast a dark shadow over anything claimed by government officials. As a result of various lies, called false flag tactics, such as the Bay of Tonkin incident used to start the Vietnam War, Americans no longer believe their politicians without question. And yet, under false flags, new wars have been started in Iraq and Afghanistan, and Americans lent support to their leaders.

History damns duplicity, but by the time history reveals subterfuge, the deed has been done. James Madison was quoted as saying, 'If tyranny and oppression come to this land, it will be in the guise of fighting a foreign enemy.'

How true, how true.

This reading is ended."

Q: Mr. Cayce, this is a long one, but a good one: Science describes emotion as being controlled by chemicals in the physical body. Being a woman who has gone through pregnancy and childbirth, as well as one who has studied the data as a psychologist, I can vouch for the truth in what is described by scientists. However, from patients who have (died and) "come back" from the other side, we hear of tremendous emotion: joy, peace, anger, fear...the list is actually rather long. Many scientists have studied this in order to disprove these (after-death) experiences—after all, they question, how is emotion possible without a physical body to control it? What is the truth concerning emotion beyond the physical world? How do the theories of metaphysical dualism come into play? They must, must they not? Do physical properties—the brain and its chemicals and the firing of synapses—truly control emotion? Or is emotion a completely different thing still in existence beyond the realm of the physical?

A: "Do not confuse emotion with judgment. The mind is reason; emotion is sensory. An aroma can evoke emotion. Music, the odor of a puppy, flowers, the scent of citrus, may bring back memories or titillate an olfactory response. These sensory responses to sounds and scents are the physical reactions brought about by the firing of synapses, as you put it. Without the physical body the entity does not have the ability to react to the physical stimuli. But let us define emotion. Feeling something without benefit of identifiable cause—that is unadulterated emotion.

Therefore, faith, sympathy, patriotism, or symmetry of dance with sensuous moves can bring about an intellectual response that we might deem as emotion.

Emotion in the physique is a vibratory reaction from one portion of the body to another. Emotion can be a glandular response provoked by gonads, spleen, or thyroid sending signals to the brain. All of this is in the three-dimensional world of the Earth plane. A scientist reasons that without the physical body there could be no joy, sense of peace, anger, or fear.

He is correct on the physical plane.

It is the yearning for those emotions that lures an entity back from the Universal Wave to endure the angst and agonies of life on Earth. As a spirit, the entity remembers sensations fondly in the same way living entities are drawn to fast automobiles or dangerous mountain peaks in search of adrenalin that makes them feel 'alive.'

Does this mean that there is no emotion in the spirit world? Yes, as indicated, he feels no fear, anger, or other destructive impulses. What he does feel, are tragedies of war, peace, and serenity, and the comfort of physical freedom. Like a fledgling bird taking first flight, the wind in pinfeathers, the buoyancy of soaring, the newly-arrived spirit zips about the universe in complete abandon. It is fun. It also gets old. The entity begins to think of the physical world with its tactile sensations of sex, the fervor of hatred, the tranquility of lazy afternoons in a summer hammock. Is that not emotion?

Gazing upon the physical world and seeing tragedies of war and disease, a spirit is cloaked in sad empathy. That is emotion, isn't it?

The birth of a healthy child, at the point where he sheds the fourth level of awareness, he is the embodiment of innocence, if only for a little while. This is cause for joy, and that is an emotion.

There are two kinds of emotion: the glandular and chemical stimulus of the physical plane, the purely sentient cause and effect of impetus and response. Then there is the metaphysical reaction, more difficult to comprehend without the fourth level of awareness that is lost upon birth into the Earth plane. The spirit emotion is nevertheless emotion. It is rectified by an overview of the world and its inhabitants. With the joy of a baby's healthy birth there is also the awareness of troubles that will eventually come, of failures, pains and disappointments, loves lost and ambitions thwarted. Knowing the inevitability of future unhappiness, the observing spirit feels sadness mixed with the natal joy. That is emotion.

Be wise in your lifetime. Seize upon the good days and relish them. Bask in pleasures of the flesh. Absorb the affection of fellow beings. Love and be loved, caress and be caressed. Take every peaceful moment as a treasure to be enjoyed and never trivialized, because luck's a chance and trouble's sure.

And yet, in troubled times, remember these traumas will pass. Endure misfortune with philosophic forbearance. Good experiences are memories to be stored for less happy times. In the midst of turmoil and pain, summon those joyful reminiscences and remember—this will pass.

Of all the animals, only Man is born knowing he will eventually die. That is precious knowledge not to be squandered. This means every experience should be treasured, good or bad. Make the most of the physical sojourn. You are here by choice. This is what you wanted. Appreciate the experience, value the instant, and emphasize the growth that comes out of adversity and loss.

Pray not for what you want, but that God's will be done on Earth as it is in heaven. Pray for others. Say to God, 'If it is Your heavenly purpose, please help this unfortunate soul...' and every day give thanks for your blessings, peace, health, and prosperity.

Recognize the celestial and universal system of life, the majesty of creation and the masterful strokes bestowed upon us by the Creator.

Scientists describe the beginning of the universe as the Big Bang, and they are correct. God said, 'Let there be light,' and (bang!) there was light.

You do not have to flaunt your faith to be religious. It is not necessary to proselytize in search of errant souls—they will find their way in time. Concentrate on self. Build the temple that is within you.

Welcome others, but do not feel you must drag them

into awareness against their will.

Many sins have been perpetrated in the name of religion. Oratory and bombast are not proof of sincerity. Quiet personal faith is no less a monument to the glory of God. Give thanks. Show that you recognize and admire what He has done on our behalf.

And yes, do it with emotion.

One does not have to be psychic to predict some of what is coming in this century. Severe weather that once occurred every fifty years will become more intense and will recur every ten years. There will be more hurricanes and tornadoes, each disturbance progressively more devastating than storms of decades past. By the time this entity takes a breath in the year 2050, the world will be assailed by increasingly damaging meteorological events. Corporations and pundits with selfish agendas will claim these are normal historical cycles that have come about in centuries past. They are right. Similar cycles have caused ice ages and centuries of tropical heat.

The difference this time is that the natural course of ocean currents and atmospheric responses has been unbalanced by activities of mankind. Before fragile equilibrium is reestablished there will be decade after decade of increasingly ferocious storms. Concurrently, as the globe adjusts to the new mix of overheated summers and more frigid winters, there will be an increase in earthquakes and tidal waves, and sea levels will rise.

With every cold month, cynics will say this proves there is no global warming. In fact, colder winters are a direct result of diminished ozone and warmer summers; consider deserts, which scorch by day and freeze at night.

Do not be afraid. Put your faith in God and trust in the ingenuity of Man to find ways to overcome abuses to the environment. Adapt, as has been herein described. Look not to government or corporate entities for solutions, but to yourself as a first step to correct errors of the past.

Do not waste anything; not your time or energy, nor resources that today you use and discard. Especially, do not waste the precious treasure of love. Each day in every way act in a manner that will not embarrass you upon return to the Universal Wave where every entity sees you clearly.

Be kind.

Be gentle.

Be generous to those less blessed than you.

Love your spouse and the children you've gotten. Forgive the youthful transgressions young people are prone to make.

Forgive your parents for mistakes they have made. It is not easy to be a mother or father. We all err; nobody is perfect.

Meditate and pray. Let the Creator know how grateful you are for all that He has done for you. If He is guilty of a misstep, remember that even God can make a mistake. Forgive Him.

Forgive yourself.

Make the world happy to have had the pleasure of your company.

Man will survive.

So will you."